Navigating the Shadows: Your Guide to the Dark Web

In a digital world where information travels at the speed of light and transparency is the mantra of the day, the allure of anonymity creates an intriguing paradox. Welcome to the "Dark Web," a hidden realm of the internet shrouded not in mystery, but in uncharted potential. This book is your guide to that enigmatic corner of the online world— an exploration of the unindexed, the anonymous, and sometimes, the infamous aspects of the internet.

"The Dark Web" is often misunderstood and steeped in myth, sometimes portrayed as a virtual den where only illegal and illicit activities occur. While it's true that the Dark Web harbors space for illicit exchanges, there lies within it a landscape for free expression, a haven for those in search of privacy, and essential tools for those evading censorship in oppressive regimes.

This guide seeks to demystify the Dark Web and provide you with a clear, insightful, and secure approach to understanding and navigating this complex environment. We'll journey through the Dark Web origins, explore its structures, delve into its use and misuse, and equip you with the tools you need to engage with it safely and responsibly. Embrace the shadows with eyes wide open; your journey into the depths begins here.

Table of Contents

10. Academia's Role in Shaping the Future of the Dark Web

- Understanding User Behavior
- Technological Innovations
- Ethical Frameworks
- Legal Scholarship
- Interdisciplinary Approaches
- Data Privacy Concerns

11. The Private Sector (Corporate Responsibility) and Market Dynamics

- Cyber Espionage: The Invisible Battlefield
- Economic Warfare: Veils of Anonymity
- The Role of Lobbying and Special Interests: The Unseen Architects of Digital Policy
- Collateral Damage: The Unseen Toll

12. Governmental Oversight: Regulation, Surveillance, and Ethics

- Regulatory Frameworks
- Surveillance Tactics: Information Warfare
- Ethical Governance: The Delicate Balance
- International Cooperation: A Global Perspective
- Legislative Challenges: Existing Laws are Often Inadequate

13. Civil Society and Grassroots Movements: The Power of the Collective

- Advocacy and Awareness (CSOs)
- Whistleblowing Platforms
- Human Rights and the Dark Web
- Community Policing
- Educational Outreach
- Public Discourse and Policy Influence

14. Advanced Risks for Tor Users

- Advanced Exploits
- Darknet Markets and Darkcoins

Chapter 1: Introduction

In a digital world where information travels at the speed of light and transparency is the mantra of the day, the allure of anonymity creates an intriguing paradox. Welcome to the "Dark Web," a hidden realm of the internet shrouded not in mystery, but in uncharted potential. This book is your guide to that enigmatic corner of the online world—an exploration of the unindexed, the anonymous, and sometimes, the infamous aspects of the internet.

The Dark Web is often misunderstood and steeped in myth, sometimes portrayed as a virtual den where only illegal and illicit activities occur. While it's true that the Dark Web harbors space for illicit exchanges, there lies within it a landscape for free expression, a haven for those in search of privacy, and essential tools for those evading censorship in oppressive regimes.

This guide seeks to demystify the Dark Web, providing you with a clear, insightful, and secure approach to understanding and navigating this complex environment. We'll journey through its origins, explore its structures, delve into its use and misuse, and equip you with the tools you need to engage with it safely and responsibly. Embracing the shadows with eyes wide open; your journey into the depths begins here.

The concept of anonymity has been a cornerstone of human civilization since ancient times. From the ancient Greeks' use of pseudonyms to modern-day encryption methods, humans have always sought ways to conceal their identities and protect themselves from persecution. The Dark Web is an extension of this quest for anonymity, but it's essential to understand that its evolution is not solely driven by malicious intentions.

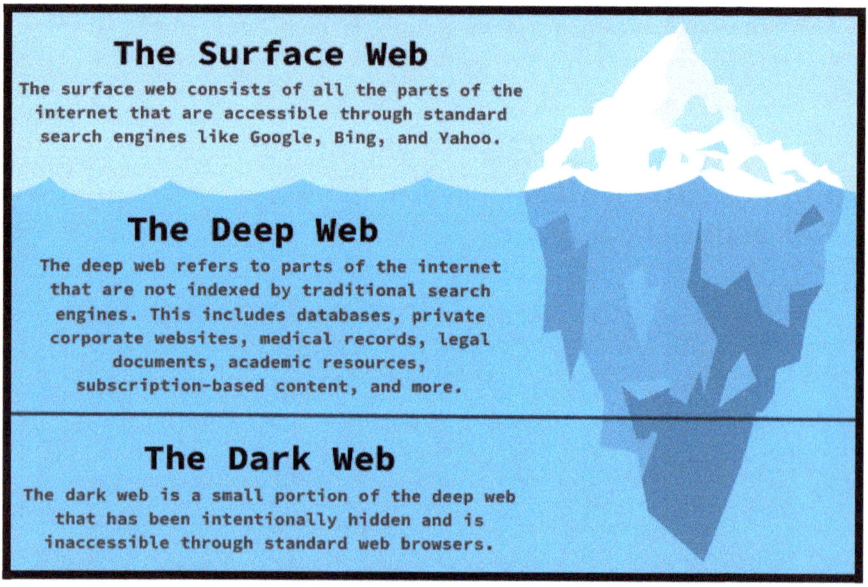

The term "Dark Web" was first coined in the 1980s by the United States Naval Research Laboratory (NSRL) as a reference to the hidden aspects of the internet. The NSRL created the precursor to the modern-day Tor network, designed to protect U.S. intelligence communications online from interception and surveillance. This project laid the groundwork for the development of more sophisticated anonymity tools.

However, it wasn't until the early 2000s that the Dark Web began to take shape as we know it today. The rise of peer-to-peer (P2P) networks and the subsequent creation of decentralized platforms like Freenet and I2P enabled users to access and share content without relying on centralized servers.

The proliferation of these technologies, coupled with advancements in encryption methods and the increasing availability of anonymity tools, created a perfect storm that would give birth to the modern Dark Web. The Silk Road, launched in 2011, is often cited as one of the first major darknet marketplaces. Its success paved the way for other similar platforms, including Black Market Reloaded and AlphaBay.

However, it's essential to note that the Dark Web is not a monolithic entity; rather, it's a complex ecosystem comprising various networks, each with its unique characteristics, risks, and use cases. The Tor network, for instance, is often mistakenly conflated with the Dark Web. While both are related, they serve distinct purposes.

The Tor network is primarily designed to provide anonymity and privacy for "legitimate" users, whereas the Dark Web encompasses a broader range of activities, including illicit exchanges and malicious endeavors. Understanding this distinction is crucial for navigating the Dark Web safely and responsibly.

In the following chapters, we'll delve deeper into the intricacies of the Dark Web, exploring its evolution, risks, and opportunities. We'll examine the various networks that comprise it, discuss the tools and techniques used to access and navigate these platforms, and provide guidance on how to engage with them securely.

Before we proceed, it's essential to acknowledge that the Dark Web is a complex and ever-evolving environment. New technologies and methods are emerging daily, making it challenging to keep pace.

As your guide, I'll do my best to provide you with accurate and up-to-date information; however, it's crucial for you to remain vigilant and critically evaluate any information you encounter.

In the next chapter, we'll explore the types of websites that can be found on the Dark Web, including .onion sites, secure drop platforms, and other forms of content. We'll also discuss the risks associated with these platforms and provide guidance on how to identify and avoid them safely.

Before we proceed, please note that some of the information discussed in this book may be disturbing or uncomfortable.

A Brief History of Anonymity Online

Early Internet Days (1980s - 1990s)
In the early days of the internet, anonymity was relatively straightforward, primarily relying on pseudonyms in forums and email lists. Systems such as Usenet and early bulletin board systems (BBSs) facilitated a sense of community engagement, allowing users to communicate without revealing personal identities. The culture of these early platforms valued privacy and free expression, as users explored their interests in relative anonymity.

Rise of Encryption and Privacy Technologies
As the internet evolved, concerns over privacy and surveillance began to surface. The introduction of encryption technologies, such as Pretty Good Privacy (PGP) in 1991 by Phil Zimmermann, allowed users to encrypt their emails and files, providing a foundational layer of security and anonymity. PGP allowed users to communicate securely, but its uptake was limited due to the complexity of managing encryption keys.

The Emergence of Anonymity Networks
By the late 1990s, initiatives aimed at preserving user anonymity began to gain traction. Projects like Freenet (launched in 2000) sought to enable users to share files without revealing identities, functioning as a peer-to-peer platform. Freenet used a decentralized model, where data was stored across various nodes rather than on a central server, making it difficult to censor or survey. Although Freenet offered a measure of anonymity, it was not without usability issues and criticisms regarding efficiency.

Formation of the Tor Network (2002)
The most significant advancement for online anonymity came with the launch of the Tor network (originally "The Onion Router") in 2002. Developed by the U.S. Naval Research Laboratory, Tor was designed to protect U.S. intelligence communications online. It facilitated anonymous browsing by routing internet traffic through a series of volunteer-operated servers (nodes), effectively masking users' identities and locations. Tor allowed for the creation of .onion websites that could only be accessed through the Tor browser, establishing a hidden layer of the internet that would become synonymous with the Dark Web.

Pivotal Events

Creation of the Silk Road (2011)
Silk Road, launched in February 2011 by Ross Ulbricht under the pseudonym “Dread Pirate Roberts,” was a major turning point for the Dark Web. It became the first significant online marketplace allowing users to buy and sell illegal goods, primarily drugs, using Bitcoin as the currency of exchange. Silk Road utilized Tor to provide anonymity and a ratings system to build trust between buyers and sellers. Its success highlighted the potential of the Dark Web for illicit commerce

and drew massive media attention.

Increased Law Enforcement Activity
As the Silk Road gained popularity, law enforcement began to take notice. FBI and DEA efforts targeted the site, leading to undercover operations to gather intelligence and apprehend Ulbricht. The first attack upon the Silk Road was the arrest of vendors and buyers in 2012 for drug trafficking. This increased scrutiny led to heightened awareness of the Dark Web among law enforcement agencies around the world.

Silk Road Shutdown (2013)
On October 1, 2013, the FBI successfully closed Silk Road and arrested its founder, Ross Ulbricht. The seizure of the Silk Road marked a significant moment in law enforcement's battle against online illicit trade. However, its closure did not eliminate the demand or the market for anonymous transactions; it simply shifted the activity to other similar platforms (e.g., Silk Road 2.0, AlphaBay).

The Birth of Successor Markets
In the wake of the Silk Road's closure, several successor markets emerged, including Silk Road 2.0 (launched shortly after the original's demise), AlphaBay, and Hansa. These new platforms utilized similar models to offer a marketplace for illicit goods, indicating the resiliency of the Dark Web economy.

High-Profile Shutdowns and Law Enforcement Alliances
The ongoing battle between law enforcement and Dark Web markets resulted in several significant operations targeting multiple marketplaces. AlphaBay, for example, was shut down in July 2017 by the FBI, and the Hansa marketplace was also taken down in a coordinated law enforcement effort. High-profile operations revealed increasing collaboration between international law enforcement agencies, leading to a more unified approach to combating

illicit activities on the Dark Web.

Shifting Landscape of the Dark Web

The Dark Web continues to evolve, shaped by technological advancements (e.g., the use of blockchain technology in financial transactions) and an increasingly sophisticated response from law enforcement. Users are now faced with a dynamic landscape where new technologies, such as AI-driven tools for tracking and analyzing Dark Web activity, threaten to complicate their access to anonymity.

Chapter 2: Understanding the Dark Web Ecosystem

The Dark Web is home to a diverse range of websites, each serving different purposes. Some are designed for legitimate use, while others are used for illicit activities. Here are some examples:

- **.onion websites (Tor)**: These are websites that can only be accessed using the Tor browser and require users to have a valid .onion domain name. They are often used for communication, information sharing, and e-commerce.

- **Secure drop platforms**: These are websites designed for secure file sharing and communication (often used for whistleblowing). They use end-to-end encryption and other security measures to protect user data.

- **Document sharing sites:** Some Dark Web platforms allow users to share documents, including sensitive information and copyrighted materials.
- **Free e-book platforms:** Some websites offer free e-books, often in formats like PDF or EPUB.

How to Access .onion Websites using Tor Browser

Accessing .onion websites requires a valid .onion domain name and the Tor browser. Here's a step-by-step guide:

1. Download and install the Tor browser from the official website.

2. Launch the Tor browser and wait for it to connect to the Tor network.

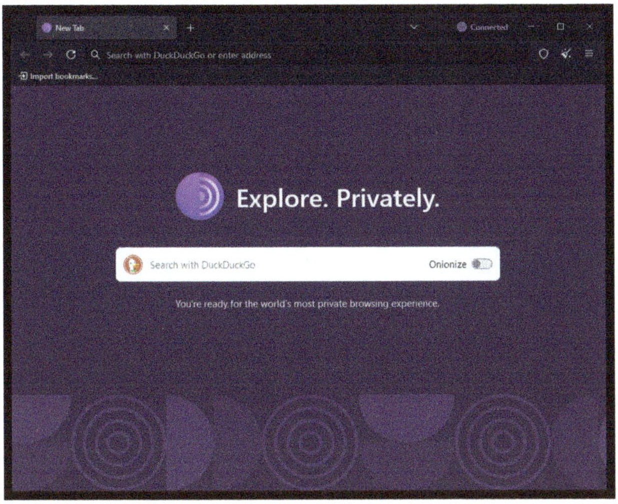

3. Enter the desired .onion URL in the address bar, replacing "www" with ".onion".

4. Click on the site to access it.

Types of Dark Web Sites

Dark Web Marketplaces

- **Archetyp Market:** A Dark Web marketplace known for a variety of illicit goods and services.

- **Bohemia Market:** A Dark Web marketplace that features various goods, including legal and illegal products.

Hacking Forums and Communities

- **Exploit.in Forum:** A forum focused on sharing hacking techniques, exploits, and cybersecurity discussions.
- **xmrguide:** A community focusing on Monero cryptocurrency and related discussions.

Anonymous Communication and Email Services

- **Protonmail:** A secure email service that emphasizes privacy and encryption.
- **Riseup:** An activist online service providing secure communications tools for activists and dissenters.

- **TorBox Email:** A service offering anonymous email communication through the Tor network.

- **Secmail:** A temporary email service designed for anonymous communications.

News and Information Outlets

- **BBC:** A version of the BBC news site, providing news articles and reports anonymously on the Dark Web.

- **ProPublica:** Investigative journalism outlet offering reports and articles focused on transparency and accountability.

- **The Intercept:** A journalism platform known for investigative reporting, particularly on government secrecy.

- **The New York Times:** A version of the mainstream news outlet that can be accessed anonymously.

Privacy and Security Tools

- **Cryptostorm VPN:** A virtual private network service focusing on privacy and security.

- **Mullvad VPN:** Another VPN service that promotes anonymity online.

- **DuckDuckGo:** A privacy-focused search engine that does not track users' searches.

- **Keybase:** A secure messaging and file-sharing platform that connects with cryptographic identities.

Cryptocurrency Related Platforms

- **Cryptostamps:** Buy postage with popular cryptocurrencies.

- **0xacab:** Described as "Code hosting for friendly people." Anonymous alternative to GitHub/GitLab/etc.

- **Blockchair:** A blockchain explorer and analytics platform for various cryptocurrencies.

- **Swp.cx:** Swap Monero and Bitcoin.

Research and Development Services

- **The Tor Project:** Resources and information related to the Tor network, promoting privacy and anonymity online.

- **The Hidden Wiki:** A wiki that provides links to various Dark Web platforms and resources. Explained more in Chapter 5.

- **Dark.fail:** Resource that provides links to various Dark Web platforms and resources. Explained more in Chapter 5.

Secure Document Sharing and Archiving

- **Archive.is**: A service for creating snapshots of web pages, preserving content over time.

- **Internet Archive:** Digital archive of the World Wide Web. Creates snapshots of web pages.

- **Distributed Denial of Secrets**: A non-profit organization focused on transparency and leaking information.

- **WikiLeaks:** Non-profit media organization and publisher of leaked documents

Miscellaneous

- **The CIA's Official Onion Site**: A hidden service for the Central Intelligence Agency providing information and resources.

- **The USA's NCIJ Task Force**: A task force related to national cybersecurity and defense. If you see a Tor website that has been seized and/or taken down, their logos are often on the website.

Overview of The Hidden Wiki

The Hidden Wiki is one of the most well-known directories on the Dark Web. It was created by an individual or group using Tor, with the intention of providing users with a safe and anonymous way to access various websites and resources. The site itself is not indexed by search engines like Google, making it difficult for law enforcement agencies to track its activity.

The Hidden Wiki provides links to various .onion sites, which are accessible only through the Tor browser. These sites range from news outlets and forums to marketplaces and services that offer a range of products and information.

The Hidden Wiki is not just a simple directory; it's a complex network of websites and resources that cater to various interests and needs. It's essential to approach this resource with caution, as some sites may contain malicious content or be used for illicit activities.

Overview of Dark.fail

Dark.fail is another directory on the Dark Web that provides links to various .onion sites. It can also serve as a valuable resource for those seeking information on specific topics or looking to explore new technologies.

Potential risks

- **Malicious content:** Some sites on the directory may contain malicious software or phishing scams.
- **Illicit activities:** The Dark Web is known for its illicit marketplaces and services, which can be accessed through The Hidden Wiki.
- **Data collection:** Law enforcement agencies may still collect data from users who visit these

sites.

Note: The references provided are for informational purposes only and should not be considered as endorsements or recommendations.

Chapter 3: Safety and Security

The Dark Web is an unforgiving environment that poses significant risks to users. As you navigate the shadows, it's essential to prioritize your safety and security above all else.

Your identity is your most valuable asset in the digital world. The Dark Web offers numerous opportunities for identity theft, financial exploitation, and other malicious activities. To protect yourself from these threats:

- **Use a VPN**: A Virtual Private Network (VPN) masks your IP address, making it difficult for hackers to track your online activity.
- **Choose a reliable VPN service**: Research reputable VPN providers that prioritize user privacy and security. Look for services with strong encryption, no-logging policies, and transparent practices.
- **Keep your software up-to-date**: Regularly update your operating system, browser, and other software to ensure you have the latest security patches and features.

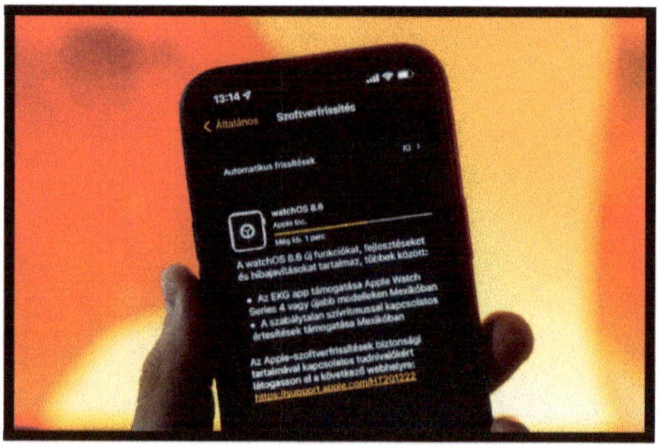

Best Practices for Choosing a Reliable VPN Service

- **No-logging policy**: Ensure the provider has a strict no-logs policy, meaning they don't store any user data.
- **Strong encryption**: Opt for services that use robust encryption protocols like AES-256 or OpenVPN.
- **Transparent practices**: Research the company's values and mission to ensure alignment with your own principles.

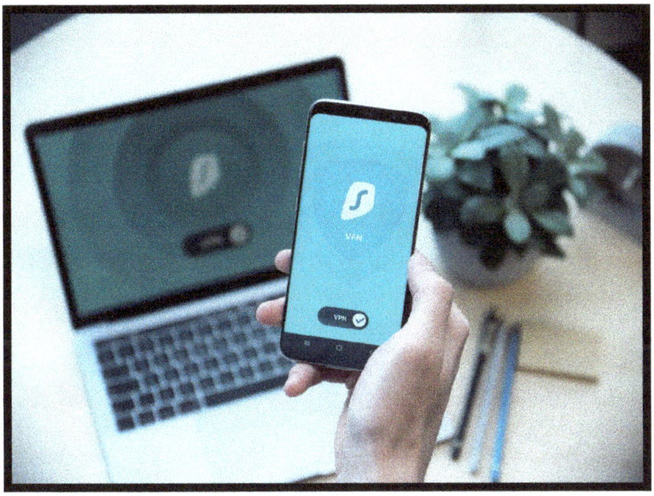

Tor Browser Settings for Maximum Anonymity

- **Use a secure operating system:** Install Tails OS, which is designed specifically for anonymous browsing.
- **Disable JavaScript:** Enable this setting in your Tor browser settings to reduce tracking and fingerprinting attempts.
- **Avoid using personal data:** Refrain from sharing sensitive information like credit card numbers or social security details.

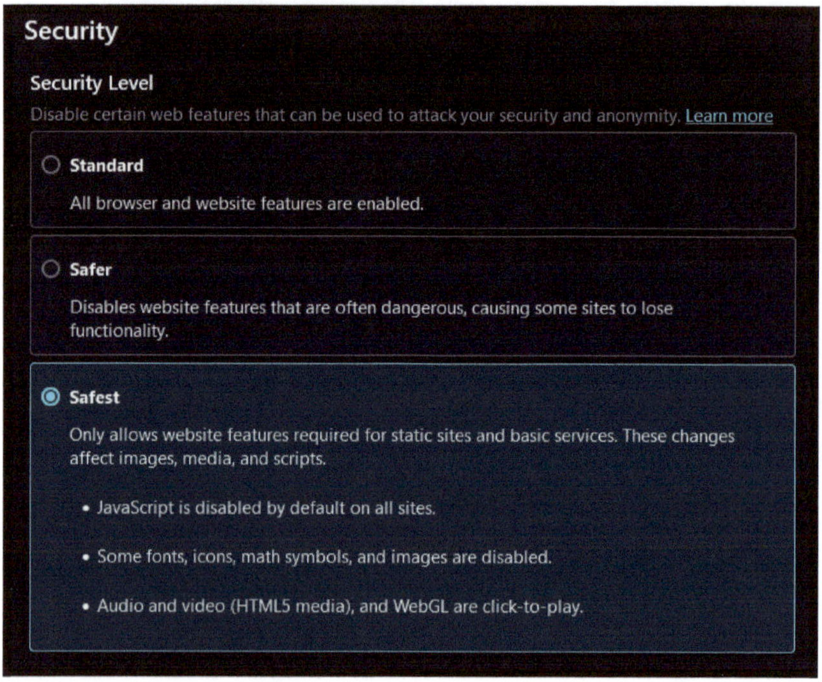

Additional Safety Measures

- **Use a secure email service**: Choose an encrypted email provider like ProtonMail or Tutanota for secure communication.
- **Be cautious with links and attachments**: Avoid clicking on suspicious links or opening malicious attachments from unknown sources.
- **Regularly back up your data**: Use encryption to protect your files and ensure you can recover them in case of a security breach.
- **Using Burner Phones:** Acquire a prepaid phone that is not linked to your identity. Use it solely for activities related to the Dark Web to reduce the risk of linking your personal information with your online actions. Burner phones can easily be discarded if the risks increase.
- **Avoid personal information:** Do not register any accounts or provide real data on the burner phone. This helps ensure that your identity remains protected.

Operational Security

- **Employing Pseudonyms:** When engaging in transactions or discussions, always adopt a pseudonym that doesn't link back to your real identity. This includes using usernames, email aliases, and even fake physical addresses when required.
- **Consistency across platforms:** Ensure that you are consistent in the identity you present across different Dark Web platforms, which adds a layer of reliability to your pseudonym.
- **Switching Laptop WiFi Cards:** Consider using

removable WiFi adapters. This can be helpful to prevent persistent tracking associated with physical hardware. When accessing the Dark Web, use a distinct adapter that isn't used for standard internet access.

- **Rotational usage:** Switch between different adapters (and locations) for different sessions, especially for accessing particularly sensitive sites to further obscure your identity.

Ordering Techniques

- **Setting Up Drop Houses for Ordering Packages:** Rent or establish drop locations for receiving packages involving sensitive transactions. This could be a temporary address or a storage facility that does not disclose your identity.

- **Avoid deliveries to your home:** Prevent any item linked to your real identity from reaching your residence, which could open doors for identification or tracking by authorities. If you must use your own address, use your real name. Do not risk them refusing to deliver the package as this will often result in them searching the package.

- **Drop Shippers:** If you find yourself ordering (or selling) frequently, consider contacting a dedicated drop shipper. USPS is less likely to search a well seasoned drop house. (Example. If you ship a lot to a particular country, find a drop shipper in that country who will forward the package for a fee)

- **Monitor Information About the Seller:** Screen the reputation and reviews of the seller or marketplace you're purchasing from. Forums and user feedback can give insights into whether others had issues, which can mitigate risks.

- **Order in Small Quantities:** If you are trying a new vendor, consider ordering smaller quantities first to gauge the reliability of their service and packaging. This will also reduce the cost should anything go wrong.

- **Timing Your Retrieval:** If using a drop or a shipping service, try to time your package retrieval at low-traffic times to reduce the chance of being seen.

Shipping Techniques

- **Utilize vacuum sealers**: For any items being shipped, especially those of a sensitive nature, vacuum sealing can reduce visibility and protect items from detection. This is often used for products that may raise suspicions if found openly.

- **Two Layer Minimum:** Always have the item packaged in an inner and an outer packaging (at the bare minimum).

- **Shipping Decoys:** Add a normal item to the outer packaging in the event a LEO (Law Enforcement Officer) opens the package. They will not typically dig all the way down to an inner package if it seems like a normal item to ship on the outside.

- **Real Return Address:** In the event the item is undelivered, include a real return address (but in a bad area of town). Do not risk having an item sent back to yourself (or to a fake address) as this will result in the package being searched.

- **Wear gloves:** Always wear gloves to prevent leaving fingerprints behind. Use gloves with minimal patterns to avoid trace evidence. Avoid colored or textured gloves that could be identified.

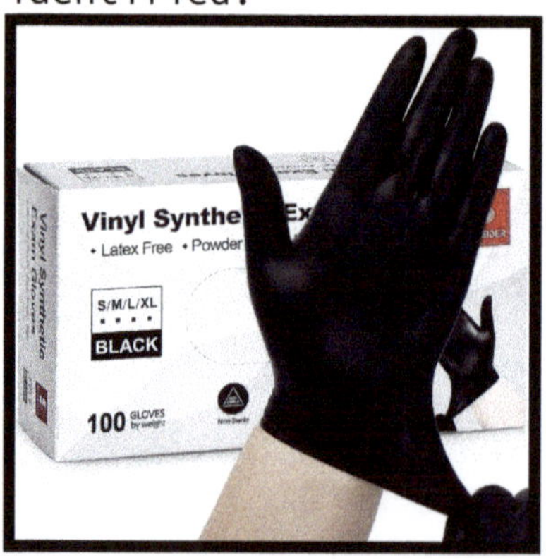

- **Hairnet & Protective Gear:** Use a hair net to avoid leaving hair follicles. Wearing a mask can also protect any trace DNA or saliva while handling items.

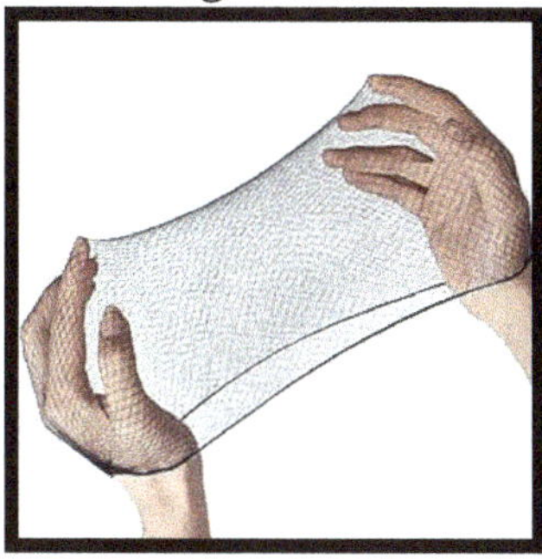
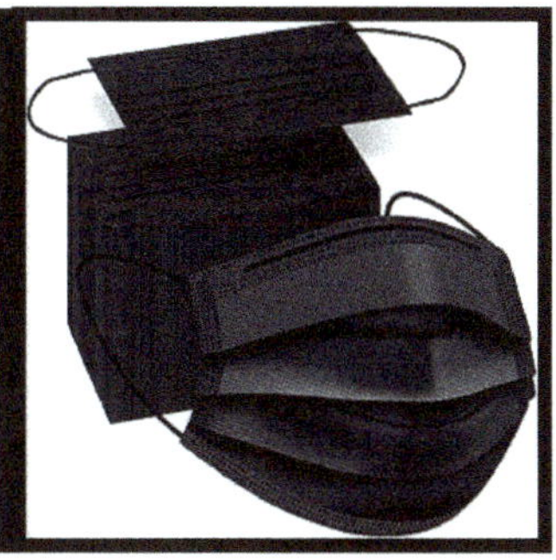

- **Cleaning items:** Anything that could carry traces of your DNA should be cleaned thoroughly with disinfectants that could eliminate biological traces before shipping.

- **Disguise the package:** Consider using unmarked packaging and avoid any labels that could reveal the shipment's contents; this helps in blending in with standard shipping. Make the package as normal looking as possible. Research the norm in your area and copy it exactly. USPS workers deal with thousands of packages, don't have yours be the only one in a green box with 100 layers of tape.

- **Utilizing Blue Boxes:** Find a good set of Blue Boxes around town, regularly rotate which box you use (or drop off smaller amounts at various ones). Boxes without cameras (such as one not directly outside of a Post Office) are best.

Using Crypto Payment Methods

- **Preferred Cryptocurrencies:** Utilize privacy-focused cryptocurrencies like Monero to facilitate payments whenever possible. Unlike Bitcoin, which is pseudonymous and can be traced, Monero provides enhanced transaction anonymity.
- **Mixers and Tumblers:** If you must use Bitcoin, consider using mixing services or tumblers that obfuscate the source of your funds by mixing them with others, making it more difficult to trace back to you.

Common Mistakes to Avoid

When navigating the Dark Web, it's easy to fall prey to common mistakes that can compromise your safety and security. Be aware of these pitfalls to avoid them:

- **Using public computers or unsecured networks without the proper precautions**: Public computers and unsecured networks are typically more vulnerable to hacking and surveillance. If you use a public place (some Dark Web users ONLY use external locations), make sure you are following the suggestions from Chapters 3 and 5
- **Sharing personal data**: Refrain from sharing sensitive information like credit card numbers, social security details, or other identifying information.
- **Clicking on suspicious links or attachments**: Avoid clicking on malicious links or opening attachments from unknown sources.

Avoiding Scams and Phishing Sites

As we navigate the Darknet, it's essential to be aware of scams and phishing sites that can compromise our anonymity and put us at risk. In this section, we'll discuss how to identify suspicious websites and links, as well as provide tips for verifying website authenticity.

Scammers often use tactics like spoofing, typosquatting, or social engineering to trick users into visiting malicious websites or clicking on phishing links. Here are some red flags to watch out for:

- **Unusual URLs**: Be cautious of URLs that seem suspicious or don't match the expected domain name.
- **Typos and grammatical errors**: Scammers often make mistakes in their attempts to impersonate legitimate sites. An example of this is phishing site "dakr.fail" instead of "dark.fail"

- **Urgency tactics:** Scams often try to create a sense of urgency, such as claiming that an account will be closed if you don't take action immediately.
- **Unusual pop-ups or ads**: Be wary of websites with excessive pop-ups or ads that seem out of place.

Tips for Verifying Website Authenticity

To avoid falling victim to scams and phishing sites, follow these tips:

1. **Verify the domain name**: Make sure the website's domain name matches the expected name.
2. **Check for HTTPS encryption**: Legitimate websites should have an "https" prefix in their URL and a lock icon in the address bar.

3. **Look for trust badges:** Reputable sites often display trust badges from organizations like SSL Trust Network or GlobalSign.

4. **Be cautious of generic greetings:** Scammers may use generic greetings instead of addressing you by your name.

5. **Don't click on suspicious links:** Avoid clicking on links that seem suspicious, especially if they're embedded in emails or pop-ups.

Verify a Website's PGP Key

1. **Obtain the Official PGP Key:**

   - Visit the official site or a reliable source (like the website's FAQ or Help section) that provides the PGP key. Look for links to the key on the website itself, as reputable sites tend to publish their keys prominently.

2. **Download the PGP Key**:

   - The PGP key is often hosted as a plain text file or can be displayed directly on the website. Copy the key block, which starts with **-----BEGIN PGP PUBLIC KEY BLOCK-----** and ends with **-----END PGP PUBLIC KEY BLOCK-----**.

3. **Import the PGP Key**:

   - Use a PGP-compatible application (such as GnuPG, Kleopatra, or an email client with PGP support) to import the public key.

4. **Verify the Fingerprint**:

   - Compare the fingerprint of the imported key with the one published on the official website. The official website should display its key's fingerprint prominently to allow users to verify it.

   - Make sure they match exactly. If they do not match, it could indicate that the key has been compromised or that you are dealing with a fake site.

5. **Check the Key's Validity**:

   - Look for additional confirmations regarding the PGP key's legitimacy using services like keyservers (e.g., https://keys.openpgp.org/). You can search for the key by email or fingerprint.

     Note: Illegal sites are unlikely to have their keys uploaded to sites like these.

- Make sure the key is associated with a legitimate identity and has not expired or been revoked.

6. **Trusted Sources**:

- If available, check for web of trust indicators or signatures on the key. This means other trusted parties have verified the key's authenticity, which can enhance trust in its validity.

- Websites like Dark.fail and The Hidden Wiki typically check the keys against the URLs they list.

7. **Stay Cautious**:

- If you cannot obtain the PGP key from the website directly or if you cannot confirm its legitimacy through independent means, exercise caution before engaging with the site, especially if it involves sensitive information or transactions.

Websites will use their PGP key to sign a message on their website (Typically shown before the login)

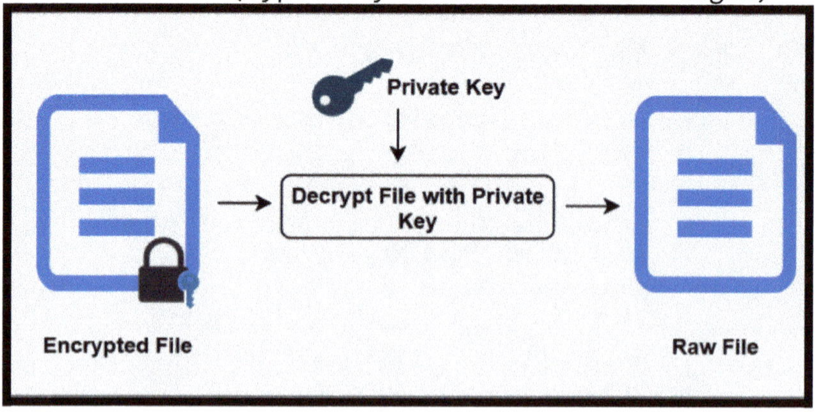

Users will decrypt/verify the signed message to confirm that the author has access to the website's PGP key

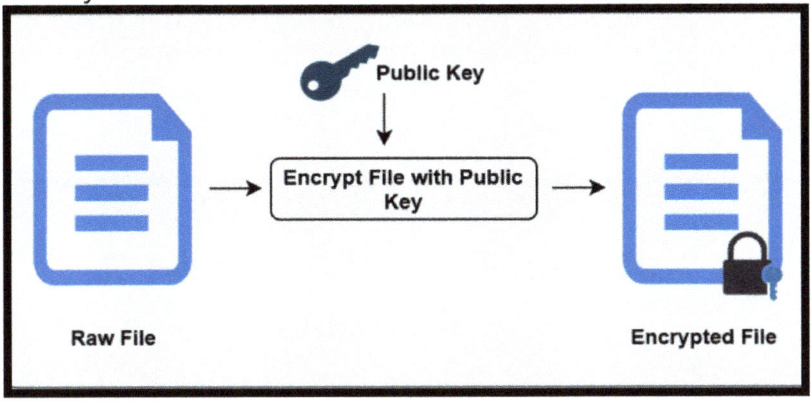

Several email providers, such as Proton shown below, have options to send/verify PGP keys

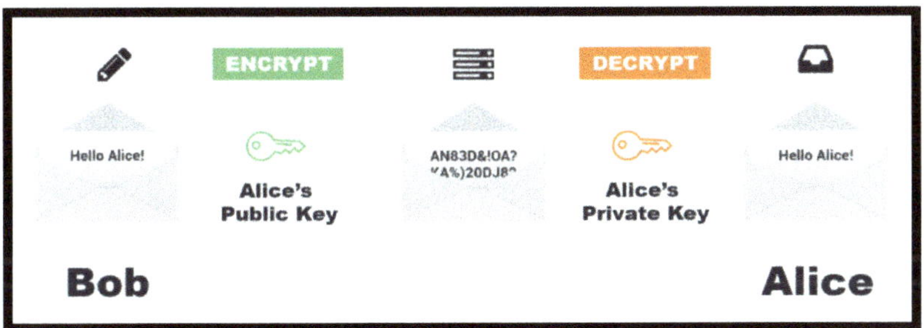

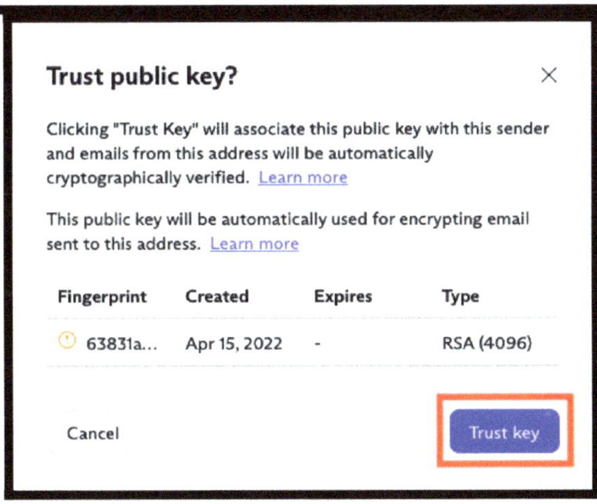

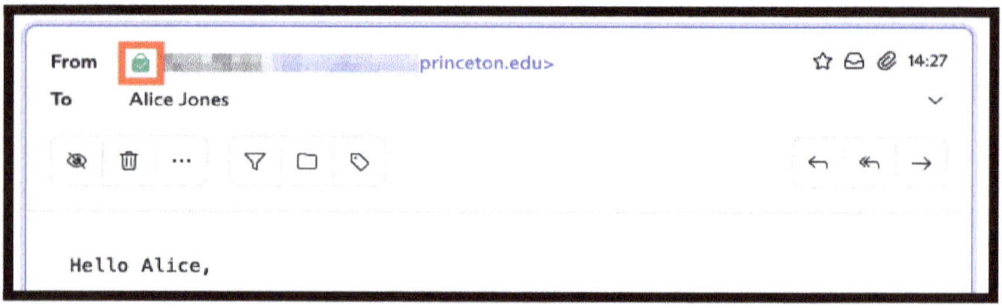

Using Temporary Email Accounts

Temporary email accounts are a great way to create a disposable email address for specific purposes without compromising your primary account. Here's how they work:

- **No setup required**: Temporary email accounts don't require any setup or personal information.
- **Short-lived**: These accounts typically expire after a short period, deleting all emails and data associated with them.

Benefits of Using Temporary Email Accounts

Temporary email accounts offer several benefits, including:

- **Anonymity**: You can create an anonymous account without revealing your real identity.
- **Disposability**: If you need to delete the account, it's gone forever, leaving no trail behind.
- **Reduced risk**: Temporary accounts reduce the risk of phishing or spamming attacks on your

primary account.

To get the most out of temporary email accounts:

- **Use a unique password**: Create a strong and unique password for each temporary account.
- **Avoid reusing passwords**: Don't reuse passwords from other accounts, as this can compromise security.
- **Keep records secure**: Store any relevant information or receipts securely to avoid losing access.

Additional Resources

For more information on avoiding scams and phishing sites, check out the following resources:

- The Tor Project's guide to staying safe online
- The Electronic Frontier Foundation's (EFF) guide to online security
- The Darknet subreddit's wiki on safety and security

By following these guidelines, you'll significantly reduce the risks associated with navigating the Dark Web. Remember that safety is an ongoing process; stay vigilant and adapt to new threats as they emerge.

Please note that some of the links provided may be subject to change or become unavailable over time. It's essential to exercise caution when accessing these resources and ensure that you have a solid understanding of the potential risks involved.

Chapter 4: Potential Consequences of Using the Dark Web

The digital world has evolved considerably, with the Dark Web emerging as a complex and often controversial segment. While it can provide anonymity and innovation, it also harbors numerous risks that can adversely affect individuals and society as a whole. This chapter aims to delve deeper into the legal implications, specific laws governing Dark Web activities, and the repercussions faced by users. Furthermore, we will emphasize the importance of being cognizant of these risks to foster a safer digital ecosystem.

Laws Regarding Dark Web Activities

The Dark Web, a subset of the Deep Web, includes websites that are not indexed by traditional search engines and typically require special software, such as Tor, to access. Here, a shadow economy thrives, with numerous illicit activities taking place. As such, understanding the laws that apply to this space is vital for anyone contemplating interaction within it.

1. Variability of Laws Across Jurisdictions

Laws governing Dark Web activities are not uniform globally. Different countries have different legal frameworks addressing cybercrime and illicit trade.

- **United States:** The U.S. has specific laws like the Computer Fraud and Abuse Act (CFAA) that criminalize unauthorized access to networks and systems, including those on the Dark Web. Additionally, various federal and state statutes target drug trafficking, human trafficking, and other crimes that may occur via hidden services.

- **European Union:** The EU has been proactive in addressing cybercrime through initiatives such as the General Data Protection Regulation (GDPR) and the Directive on Attack Against Information Systems. It maintains strict regulations around data privacy and security, which can be violated by participating in illegal activities on the Dark Web.

- **Other jurisdictions:** Countries in regions like Asia, Africa, and South America may have varying enforcement levels, with some lacking robust legal frameworks. However, the potential for international treaties and cooperation in cybercrime enforcement exists, complicating the legal landscape further.

2. Specific Illegal Activities

Several specific activities on the Dark Web are explicitly illegal, and engaging in these can attract serious legal consequences:

- **Buying or Selling Illicit Goods:** The trade of illegal substances—such as narcotics, human trafficking, counterfeit products, and stolen data—constitutes a significant portion of Dark Web transactions. Both buyers and sellers can face severe criminal charges, depending on their jurisdiction.

- **Cybercrime:** Engaging in hacking services, ransomware distribution, and id theft not only damages the victims but can also lead to lengthy prison sentences for perpetrators. Law enforcement agencies continuously evolve their tactics to combat such activities.

- **Facilitation of Criminal Behavior:** Participating in forums or groups that encourage illegal activities, even if one does not directly commit crimes, can still result in legal actions, based on conspiracy or complicity laws.

Potential Consequences of Getting Caught

The ramifications of engaging in illicit activities on the Dark Web can be severe and far-reaching. Ignorance of the law is not a defense; hence individuals must be aware of the potential consequences they may face:

1. Criminal Charges and Sentencing

Those apprehended partaking in illegal transactions on the Dark Web can face a wide array of charges, often leading to substantial prison sentences. Depending on the severity of the crime, penalties can include:

- **Felonies:** Serious crimes like trafficking drugs or weapons can lead to decades in prison and substantial fines.
- **Misdemeanors:** Less severe activities, such as simple fraud, might result in shorter jail sentences or probation but can still severely impact one's record.

2. Financial Penalties

In addition to criminal penalties, users can face significant financial repercussions. Institutions such as banks or payment processors can identify suspicious activities associated with Dark Web transactions, potentially leading to:

- **Account Freezes:** Financial accounts can be frozen permanently, disrupting one's ability to access funds or execute transactions.
- **Fines and Restitution:** Courts may impose fines that can increase if the crime involves financial gains from illicit activities. Additionally, victims may be awarded restitution requirements.

3. Reputation Damage

Being associated with the Dark Web can result in extensive damage to an individual's reputation. The stigma surrounding those involved in unlawful activities often leads to:

- **Social Ostracism:** Individuals may find themselves shunned by family, friends, and colleagues, leading to social isolation.
- **Employment Consequences:** Employers frequently conduct background checks, and a criminal record can disqualify candidates from job opportunities.

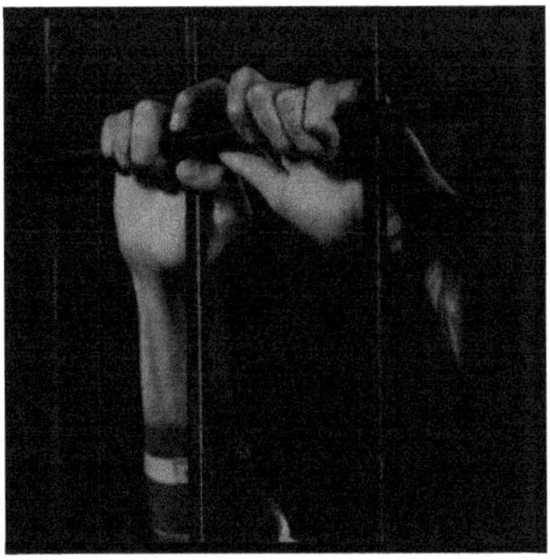

The Importance of Understanding Risks

Navigating the Dark Web safely requires a thorough understanding of the inherent risks. Individuals must educate themselves actively on their rights and legal limitations:

1. Education and Awareness

Knowledge is power, especially in the complex landscape of the Dark Web. Individuals should seek to learn about:

- Current laws and regulations: Keeping abreast of changes in laws can aid in compliance and safe navigation.
- The nature of cybercrime: Understanding how cyber perpetrators operate can help one avoid risky behaviors.

2. Utilizing Secure Communication Channels

To protect oneself while navigating the Dark Web:

- **End-to-End Encryption:** Using encrypted messaging applications ensures that communications cannot be intercepted. This protects one's identity and sensitive information.
- **VPN Services:** Virtual Private Networks can mask IP addresses, providing another layer of anonymity.

3. Avoiding Suspicious Activities

Remaining vigilant can significantly reduce the risk of entanglement in illicit activity:

- **Steering Clear of Risky Transactions:**

Individuals should refrain from engaging in dealings that feel improvisational or clandestine.

- **Trusting Reputable Sources:** Researching and utilizing trusted marketplaces or forums can minimize exposure to law enforcement and criminals.

Chapter 5: Advanced Topics in Dark Web Browsing

Secure Communication Protocols

Communication on the Dark Web is fraught with risks. The lack of regulation and oversight makes it a breeding ground for cybercriminals, hackers, and data thieves. Therefore, utilizing secure communication protocols becomes a necessity for protecting your identity and the integrity of your data.

1. Signal: An End-to-End Encrypted Messaging App

Signal is widely regarded as one of the most secure messaging applications available. It employs end-to-end encryption, ensuring that only the sender and recipient can read the messages exchanged. Even if a malicious actor intercepts the transmission, the actual content of the communication remains inaccessible without the encryption keys.

- **Features of Signal:**
  - **Self-Hosted Infrastructure:** Signal's architecture allows for user control over their data.
  - **Open Source:** Its open-source status means that security experts can audit the code for vulnerabilities, enhancing trust in the application.
  - **Multimedia:** Signal allows for the sharing of multimedia files while maintaining secure transmission

protocols.

By using Signal, users on the Dark Web can communicate confidentially and reduce the risk of exposure to surveillance or malicious attacks.

2. Bitwarden: Secure Password Management

A robust password management solution is vital for anyone interacting with the Dark Web. Bitwarden is an open-source password manager that utilizes zero-knowledge proof technology for secure information storage. This means that even Bitwarden cannot access your stored data; only you hold the key.

- **Key Features:**
    - **Password Generation:** Bitwarden can create complex, random passwords for you, eliminating the chance of user error.
    - **Encryption:** All passwords are encrypted locally before they are synced to Bitwarden's servers.
    - **Cross-Device Syncing:** Access your passwords from multiple devices without compromising security.

Effective password management not only guards

against unauthorized access but also simplifies the process of maintaining diverse, complex, and most importantly, long passwords for different accounts.

bitwarden

Tips for Creating Strong, Unique Passwords

Creating complex passwords is essential for safeguarding your online identity, particularly in a high-risk environment like the Dark Web. Here are comprehensive tips for crafting strong, unique passwords:

1. Avoid Common Patterns

Steer clear of easily guessable patterns like "123456," "password," or the use of your name and birthdate. Cybercriminals often employ dictionary attacks, which easily guess common passwords or predictable variations.

2. Incorporate Randomness

Use a mix of characters, including uppercase and lowercase letters, numbers, and special symbols to create a secure password. The randomness significantly increases the complexity, making it much harder to crack.

3. Length Matters: Understanding Password Strength

The length of a password is one of the most vital factors determining its strength. Here is a detailed breakdown of average crack times for various lengths of passwords, assuming a brute-force attack that tries every combination:

Password Length	Time to Crack (Brute Force)
6 characters	< 1 minute
8 characters	~1 hour
10 characters	~3 days
12 characters	~1 century
15 characters	~15 quintillion years

As illustrated above, longer passwords vastly increase the time required to crack them through brute-force methods. Hence, passwords should ideally exceed 12 characters in length to achieve a strong level of security.

4. Limit Reuse

Reusing passwords across different platforms creates vulnerabilities. If a password is compromised on one site, every account using the same password becomes susceptible. Always generate a unique password for each account to mitigate this risk.

Storing Sensitive Information Securely

The Dark Web is known for various marketplaces that sell sensitive information, such as credit card details or personal data. Protecting oneself from these risks involves careful storage of any sensitive information that could be exploited.

1. Use a Secure Note-Taking App

Utilize secure applications designed for storing sensitive information. Options like Tresorit and Signal are excellent choices as they prioritize security and offer end-to-end encryption for documents and notes. You should only store essential sensitive information, and nothing should reside in plaintext.

2. Enable Encryption

For any stored data—whether in cloud services or local storage—encryption is paramount. End-to-end encryption prevents unauthorized access and ensures that only intended recipients can access and decipher the stored information.

3. Limit Sharing

Only share sensitive information with trusted individuals or organizations. Even then, ensure that the communication method is secure. Avoid using public Wi-Fi networks for sharing confidential information, as these can easily be intercepted by cybercriminals.

Using a Safe Operating System

Accessing the Dark Web requires a heightened level of security and anonymity, which typically goes beyond the capabilities of traditional operating systems like Windows and macOS. While both operating systems have made strides in improving security, they are not inherently designed to provide the same level of protection that is necessary for navigating the vulnerabilities and threats endemic to the Dark Web.

Windows Spies on You

Windows operating systems, especially the more recent versions like Windows 10 and Windows 11, have garnered criticism for their privacy practices. Here are some ways in which Windows potentially collects data on users:

1. **Telemetry Data Collection**: Windows collects telemetry data, which includes information about system performance, app usage, and hardware configurations. This data is used to improve the user experience but can also be seen as intrusive.

2. **User Activity Data**: Windows may track user activities, such as the applications installed, habits, and usage patterns through features like Activity History. This information is sometimes used for personalized advertising.

3. **Cortana and Search Data**: When users engage with Cortana, Microsoft's virtual assistant, or use the Windows search feature, data about searches and interactions is collected to improve services but can also be sent back to Microsoft servers.

4. **Microsoft Account Integration**: Linking your Windows account with a Microsoft Account allows the syncing of settings and preferences, but it also tends to increase data sharing between your devices and Microsoft's servers.

5. **Advertising ID**: Windows uses an Advertising ID to track users across applications and services for the purpose of targeted advertising. Users can disable this feature, but it is enabled by default.

6. **Location Services**: Windows can collect

location data, which is used for features like location-based services and recommendations. This can be turned off in settings, but it is enabled by default for many applications.

7. **Browser Tracking**: Microsoft Edge (and other browsers) can track browsing habits and interactions for the purpose of personalized advertising and recommendations. The use of the online services is tied to your Microsoft Account.

8. **Background Apps**: Many applications in Windows are allowed to run in the background and may collect data about usage, even when the app isn't actively in use.

9. **Recall + Copilot:** Windows 11 (and some updates of 10) have a feature which utilizes regular screenshots of your screen (and an AI that looks through them) to allow users to search and retrieve past activities on their PC.

    - In the event your PC is looked through, this will have a full record of **everything** you've done on your Windows computer since installation.

macOS Spies on You

1. **Data Collection**:

    - **Telemetry & Analytics**: macOS collects system and usage data for improving user experience, which might be shared with Apple. Users can manage certain aspects of this data collection through privacy settings, but not all data collection can be completely disabled.
    - **User Behavior Tracking**: Apple may collect data related to app usage, feature adoption, and system performance

to enhance service reliability and development.

2. **iCloud and Syncing**:

    - **iCloud Syncing**: By using iCloud, users may unknowingly allow Apple to access their files, photos, and other personal data stored on the cloud. While iCloud provides conveniences, it introduces a potential privacy concern.

    - **Find My Mac**: Features like Find My Mac require location tracking, leading to continuous data collection related to location.

3. **Privacy and Security Settings**:

    - Apple's built-in privacy and security settings typically require user consent to enable features, but many users may not be fully aware of these settings or how to properly configure them to maximize privacy.

4. **App Permissions**:

    - Apps on macOS often ask for permissions to access various system components like the camera, microphone, location services, and contacts. Users may grant these permissions without fully realizing the implications.

5. **Safari and Tracking**:

    - Safari, Apple’s web browser, has features for tracking protection, but it still collects some data for personalized functions and service improvements. Some might find this unsettling as they may prefer complete anonymity while browsing.

Understanding Tails and Qubes OS

1. Tails OS

Tails, which stands for "The Amnesic Incognito Live System," is a live operating system designed for privacy and anonymity. It is a security-focused Linux distribution that runs from a USB stick or DVD, leaving no trace on the computer you're using. Tails automatically routes all internet connections through the Tor network, providing an effective means of anonymizing your online activity.

Key Features of Tails:

- **Live System**: Tails does not store data persistently; every time you boot it up, it operates in a fresh state, ensuring that no traces of your activity remain.
- **Integration with Tor**: Tails is pre-configured to connect to the Tor network, providing inherent anonymity for your browsing activities.
- **Anonymity Features**: Tails includes several privacy tools, such as a secure messaging application and a file encryption utility.
- **Software Management**: It comes with pre-installed applications like the Tor Browser, Pidgin for instant messaging, and GnuPG for

encrypting files and emails.

2. Qubes OS

Qubes OS is a security-focused operating system that utilizes virtualization technology to compartmentalize different tasks and applications. It allows users to create separate virtual environments (known as qubes) that isolate activities, providing enhanced security. In Qubes OS, even if one qube is compromised, the others remain secure, significantly mitigating the risk of data breaches.

Key Features of Qubes OS:

- **Security through Isolation**: Each application runs in its individual qube, so a compromise in one qube does not affect the others.
- **Disposable Qubes**: Users can create temporary qubes for untrusted activities, which can be deleted after use to ensure no data is left behind.
- **Template-Based Approach**: Qubes allows you to create templates for different qubes, streamlining the installation of software and maintenance processes.
- **Diverse Networking Options**: Qubes can be configured to route traffic through Tor and other secure networks, enhancing privacy while

online.

Installation Procedures

Installing Tails OS

Installing Tails OS is straightforward, and the following steps will guide you through the process:

Prerequisites:

- A USB stick (minimum 8 GB).
- A computer with access to the internet.
- A working computer to create the USB installer.

Step-by-step Instructions:

1. **Download Tails OS:**
   - Visit the Tails official website.
   - Download the latest version of Tails. You should verify the integrity of the downloaded file by following the instructions provided on the download page.
2. **Create Tails USB Stick:**
   - Use a tool such as Etcher, Rufus, or the Tails Installer to create a bootable USB stick.
   - If you are using Windows, run the Etcher application and select the Tails ISO file you downloaded. Choose your USB stick as the target drive, and click "Flash!" to create the bootable USB.
3. **Booting from the USB:**
   - Insert the Tails USB stick into the

computer you wish to use.

- Restart the computer and enter the boot menu (this is usually done by pressing a function key like F12, ESC, or DEL during startup).
- Select the USB drive from the boot options and press Enter.

4. Configure Tails Settings:

- When Tails loads, you will be prompted to configure certain settings such as language and region. You can also modify the Tor connection settings if needed.
- After configuration, click "Start Tails."

5. Navigating Tails:

- Once Tails has booted, you will be presented with the Tails desktop environment. You can use the Tor Browser to start browsing the Dark Web anonymously.
- Remember, all data is wiped after shutting down Tails, ensuring that your online activities are not recorded.

Installing Qubes OS

Installing Qubes OS requires a bit more effort due to its virtualization nature. Below are the steps for installation:

Prerequisites:

- A compatible computer (check Qubes compatibility here).
- A USB stick (minimum 16 GB).

- An internet connection for downloading the installation files.

Step-by-step Instructions:

1. **Download Qubes OS:**
    - Go to the Qubes OS official website.
    - Download the latest version of Qubes OS.
2. **Create a Bootable USB Stick:**
    - Use the same method as for Tails to create a bootable USB, utilizing tools like Etcher, Rufus, or dd (on Linux).
    - Select the Qubes ISO file you downloaded as the source file and choose your USB stick as the target.
3. **Booting from the USB:**
    - Insert the USB stick into the target computer.
    - Restart the computer and enter the boot menu by pressing F12, ESC, or DEL.
    - Select the USB drive to launch the Qubes OS installer.
4. **Install Qubes OS:**
    - Follow the on-screen instructions to install Qubes OS. You will be prompted to create the installation medium, partitions, and select disk size (minimum requirements vary).
    - The installer will guide you through selecting the installation options, including disk partitions and whether to use the default template or create your

own.

5. **Initial Boot and First Configuration:**
   - After the installation is complete, remove the USB stick and reboot the computer.
   - Upon the first boot, you will be taken to the Welcome Screen. Make sure to set a strong password for the administrative account.

6. **Setting Up Your Qubes:**
   - Once logged in, you will find yourself in the Qubes Manager, where you can create and manage multiple qubes.
   - You can start creating qubes for specific tasks (e.g., a qube for web browsing, another for document editing) and customize their settings.

7. **Routing Traffic Through Tor:**
   - To use Tor within Qubes OS, create a Tor qube that routes all traffic through the Tor network. This can be done by modifying networking settings in the Qubes Manager.

Chapter 6: The Future of Anonymity

The concept of anonymity has been a cornerstone of the Dark Web since its inception, shaping not just user interactions but also the very architecture of sites and marketplaces that thrive in obscurity. As technology evolves, so too will the methodologies and tools employed to uphold this veil of secrecy. This chapter endeavors to explore the role of cryptocurrencies in facilitating Dark Web operations, the emergence of sophisticated encryption techniques, and the nuanced future of anonymity in a rapidly changing global landscape.

The Role of Cryptocurrencies in the Dark Web

Cryptocurrency as a Currency of Choice
Cryptocurrencies have emerged as pivotal currency affecting transactions on the Dark Web. Unlike traditional currencies, cryptocurrencies enable users to conduct transactions without disclosing their identities or allowing for easy tracking (excluding Bitcoin). As a result, cryptocurrencies such as Monero have become the preferred monetary units within this hidden realm due to their inherent privacy features.

Dual-Edged Sword of Anonymity
The anonymity offered by cryptocurrencies is a double-edged sword. While they effectively shield users from conventional financial tracking, they also invite scrutiny and regulatory measures. For instance, Bitcoin transactions, while pseudonymous, can be subjected to forensic analysis that could potentially unveil the identities behind wallet addresses through cluster analysis or other

methodologies. Conversely, cryptocurrencies like Monero and Zcash utilize advanced privacy technologies that obfuscate transaction details even further, posing serious challenges for law enforcement agencies aiming to trace illicit activities.

Operational Hurdles

The inherent volatility of cryptocurrencies can present operational hurdles for Dark Web marketplaces. Price fluctuations can create instability and complicate business models that depend on consistent transactional value. Additionally, the decentralized nature of cryptocurrencies requires users to remain vigilant against hacking exploits, vulnerabilities in blockchain technology, and phishing scams. Despite these complications, the reliance on cryptocurrencies in the Dark Web's economy is unlikely to wane anytime soon; as governmental regulations intensify, Dark Web users will continue to seek out innovative methods to safeguard their financial anonymity.

Advanced Encryption Methods

Evolution of Encryption Techniques
With increasing awareness of potential surveillance and breaches within the digital space, advanced encryption methods have gained prominence as vital tools for users on the Dark Web. These sophisticated techniques are crafted to protect identities and maintain user anonymity.

Notable Encryption Examples:

- **Zero-Knowledge Proofs (ZKP):** This cryptographic method allows one party to prove the validity of a statement without disclosing any information beyond the verification itself. In the context of the Dark Web, ZKP can bolster user anonymity by verifying transactions and identities without exposing sensitive data.

- **Homomorphic Encryption:** This pioneering approach enables computations to be carried out on encrypted data, allowing for data processing without needing to decrypt it. This technology could revolutionize data exchanges on the Dark Web by facilitating secure transactions, even when intermediaries are involved.

- **Distributed Ledger Technology (DLT):** Unlike conventional ledgers, DLT records transactions across multiple participants. This enhances security by eliminating single points of failure and makes it increasingly difficult for authorities to manipulate or control data. As DLT gains traction, it may facilitate decentralized marketplaces that can resist shutdowns or interventions by law enforcement.

The complexity of these technologies may

inadvertently alienate individuals who lack the technical skills necessary to navigate them effectively, thus creating a dichotomy between seasoned users and novices on the Dark Web.

The Role of Social Engineering in the Dark Web

Social engineering, the psychological manipulation of individuals to elicit confidential information or persuade them to perform actions that compromise security, remains one of the most insidious tactics employed by cybercriminals. The Dark Web serves as a haven for social engineers, providing them access to various platforms and tools that facilitate these manipulative strategies.

Emerging Threats:

- **AI-Generated Phishing Emails**: Cybercriminals utilize machine learning algorithms to create highly personalized and convincingly crafted phishing emails that mimic trusted entities, enhancing the likelihood of information disclosure.

- **Deepfakes**: Advances in synthetic media allow attackers to create realistic audio and video deepfakes. These tools can be used to impersonate colleagues, family members, or authority figures, coercing victims into disclosing sensitive data or performing actions that breach security protocols.

- **Social Media Manipulation**: AI facilitates deception on social media platforms, propagating misinformation and propaganda. Sophisticated algorithms can generate fake accounts and content designed to mislead users, sow discord, or manipulate public opinion.

The intertwining of social engineering tactics with AI capabilities raises the stakes significantly. Individuals and organizations must remain aware of these risks and vigilant against increasingly sophisticated ploys.

Advanced Threat Protection Measures

To combat these sophisticated threats, organizations must adopt advanced threat protection measures that extend beyond traditional security approaches. A multifaceted strategy can help defend against AI-assisted social engineering attacks.

Key Measures:

- **AI-Powered Threat Intelligence**: Organizations can utilize AI-driven threat intelligence solutions to monitor patterns of malicious activity on the Dark Web effectively, analyzing vast amounts of data in real-time to discern emerging threats.
- **Behavioral Analysis:** Sophisticated behavioral analysis tools can establish baselines for normal user behavior, flagging anomalies that

may suggest nefarious activities, such as unusual login attempts or irregular changes in user patterns.

- **Machine Learning-Based SIEM Systems:** Advanced Security Information and Event Management (SIEM) systems harness machine learning algorithms to analyze log data for irregularities, providing organizations with real-time threat detection capabilities.
- **AI-Powered Incident Response:** Developing responsive incident management systems enabled by AI can facilitate rapid reactions to emerging threats, providing automated assessments of breaches and implementing containment measures.
- **Collaboration and Information Sharing:** A collaborative approach among law enforcement, security researchers, and industry experts is vital for effective intelligence sharing and best practices dissemination. By exchanging insights and trends, stakeholders can bolster their defenses against AI-driven threats.

Additional Considerations

As the integration of AI continues to evolve, organizations must also consider the broader implications:

- **AI Ethics and Regulation**: Addressing the ethical implications of AI development and its malicious uses is vital. Policymakers must create robust regulatory frameworks governing the use of AI technologies and the repercussions of their abuse in environments like the Dark Web.
- **Continuous Education and Training**: Regular training that emphasizes recognizing AI-powered social engineering attempts equips employees with the necessary skills to respond judiciously.
- **User Awareness Campaigns**: Organizations should launch campaigns aimed at raising awareness about AI-powered social engineering tactics, cultivating a culture of vigilance that encourages skepticism of unsolicited communications.

The Future of Anonymity in a Changing World

As the digital landscape continues to evolve, so too will the strategies and technologies that underpin anonymity on the Dark Web. The future of anonymity holds both promise and peril, characterized by trends that may significantly reshape the approaches individuals and organizations take towards online security and privacy.

Potential Challenges Ahead:

- **Quantum Computing**: As research in quantum

computing progresses, existing encryption algorithms may soon become vulnerable. The ability of quantum computers to solve complex mathematical problems at unprecedented speeds could undermine the security frameworks that many current privacy tools rely upon, challenging the very foundation of online anonymity.

- **Artificial Intelligence**: The deployment of AI-driven technologies presents dual-edged implications for anonymity. While AI can enhance privacy protection mechanisms, it can also be leveraged to detect and disrupt encrypted communications across the Dark Web. Predictive algorithms trained on behavioral patterns may allow for surveillance capacities that threaten user anonymity.

- **Biometric Authentication**: The increasing reliance on biometric identification methods, such as facial recognition and voice prints, poses significant threats to online anonymity. If individuals can be identified by their biological traits, the core essence of the Dark Web could be undermined.

Chapter 7: Quantum Computing and Its Implications for Encryption

Quantum computing represents a radical departure from classical computing, leveraging the principles of quantum mechanics to process information in ways that traditional computers cannot. As research in this field progresses, the implications for cybersecurity and existing encryption algorithms are profound. Current encryption methods, which form the backbone of data privacy and security on the internet, may soon face unprecedented vulnerabilities due to the computational capabilities of quantum computers.

Understanding Qubits and Encryption Vulnerabilities

At the heart of quantum computing lies the concept of the qubit (quantum bit), the fundamental unit of quantum information. Unlike classical bits, which can be either 0 or 1, qubits can exist in a state of superposition, allowing them to represent multiple states simultaneously. This property enables quantum computers to perform complex calculations at astonishing speeds.

The vulnerability of encryption methods to quantum attacks largely hinges on the number of qubits required to break them:

- **RSA Encryption**: Widely used for securing data transmission, RSA relies on the difficulty of factoring large prime numbers. Classical computers would find it infeasible to factor a 2048-bit RSA key. However, quantum algorithms like Shor's Algorithm can achieve this in polynomial time. It is estimated that approximately **2048 qubits** would be necessary for breaking a typical 2048-bit RSA key. Estimates suggest this may range from **5,000 to 15,000 physical qubits**, depending on the error rates of the quantum computers.

- **Elliptic Curve Cryptography (ECC)**: This method, favored for its strong security with smaller key sizes, utilizes the mathematics of elliptic curves. It is believed that breaking ECC with a security level equivalent to 256-bit RSA would require around **256 qubits**. Just like with RSA, the actual number of physical qubits required would be higher considering the error correction needed, potentially amounting to **1,000 to 5,000 physical qubits**, based on the specific quantum error rates and the architectures of quantum computers.
- **AES Encryption**: Advanced Encryption Standard (AES), a symmetric encryption standard, is somewhat more resilient to quantum attacks, but it is not immune. Grover's Algorithm can provide a quadratic speedup for brute-force attacks, reducing the effective key length. To effectively break AES-256 encryption, **somewhere between 3,000 and 7,000 logical qubits** would be required due to the reduced effectiveness of the key space.

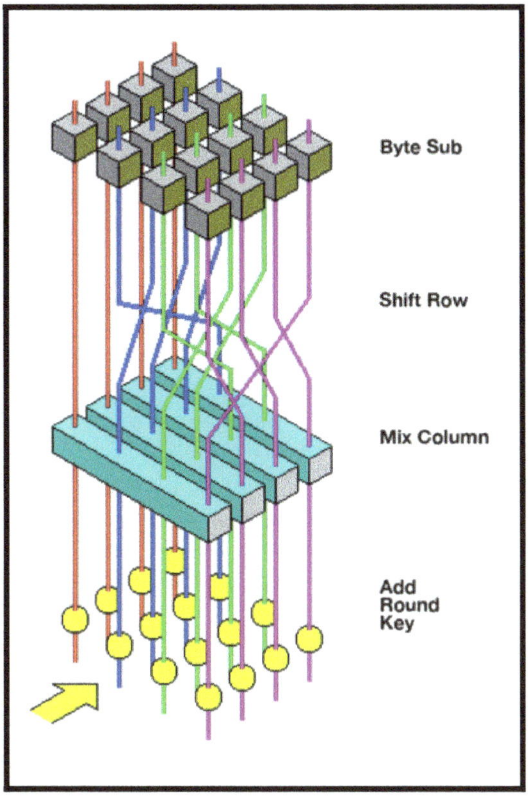

Post-Quantum Cryptography

In anticipation of the quantum threat, researchers are developing new cryptographic algorithms that are explicitly designed to be secure against quantum attacks. These algorithms will require significant advancements in classical computing to implement effectively, as well as a reevaluation of the cryptographic standards currently in use.

The rapid advances in quantum computing technology, however, challenge the viability of these existing methods, necessitating urgent discourse around the readiness of algorithms to resist quantum threats.

The Quantum Computing Landscape: Do Governments Already Have Quantum Computers?

While many governments publicly claim to be in the early stages of quantum computing development, there is speculation that significant advancements may have already been made behind closed doors.

- **Government Investments**: Various reports indicate that governments, particularly the U.S., China, and the European Union, have invested heavily in quantum research. The United States' National Quantum Initiative Act of 2018 allocated over $1.2 billion to support research in quantum technologies. China's aggressive advancements in quantum communications and computing have led to the establishment of quantum satellite systems that demonstrate tangible capabilities.
- **Declassified NSA Documents**: The National Security Agency (NSA) has declassified documents over recent years detailing its interest in quantum computing. In a 2015 report, the NSA acknowledged that "quantum computing has the potential to affect cryptography and data security on a global scale." Moreover, the agency has been researching not only quantum computing but also its implications for cryptography. This declassified information indicates that government agencies are not only monitoring quantum developments but actively engaging with them.
- **Speculative Technological Developments**: There have been rumors and speculative discussions

surrounding the existence of operational quantum hardware that could potentially be utilized for practical cryptographic attacks. While definitive proof remains elusive, the pace of technological advancements within the public and private sectors fuels speculation about what entities might possess this technology in secrecy.

Implications for Privacy and Online Anonymity

The existential threat that quantum computing poses to current encryption methods significantly undermines the security frameworks on which online anonymity and privacy depend. The potential for quantum computers to crack widely-used encryption algorithms means that sensitive information, including banking data, personal communications, and health records, could fall into the hands of malicious actors.

- **Degradation of Trust:** As encryption becomes increasingly vulnerable, trust in digital communications, e-commerce, and even healthcare data management may erode. Users could become more hesitant to share sensitive information, knowing that their data is at risk. The ramifications could extend to social media platforms and digital ecosystems where user anonymity is already a contentious subject.

- **Need for Preemptive Action**: The urgency of transitioning to post-quantum cryptographic solutions cannot be overstated. Failing to act promptly may lead organizations to remain reliant on outdated cryptographic systems, rendering them vulnerable when quantum computers become widely operational.

- **International Cybersecurity Landscape**: The development of robust quantum technologies could shift the global balance of power, particularly if certain nations gain an edge over others in quantum capabilities. As such, international cooperation in the realm of cybersecurity, standards, and protocols against quantum threats will be vital.

If IBM has a machine with **>1,121 qubits**, and the US government has been researching the technology since "2015," you can rest assured that they have the ability to crack virtually all current encryption methods. However, would they utilize something that expensive for a normal user of the Dark Web? Likely not.. for now.

Chapter 8: The Intersection with Other Online Communities

As we delve deeper into the complexities of the Dark Web, it becomes increasingly evident that its boundaries are not as rigidly defined as they may appear. The interactions and influences of the Dark Web extend far beyond its own digital realm, intersecting with various online communities in multifaceted ways. Understanding these intersections can provide valuable insights into how information flows, communities form, and digital ideologies evolve.

The Role of Social Media Platforms

Social media platforms have become integral to modern life, serving as vital arenas for information dissemination, social interaction, and community building. However, their relationship with the Dark Web is anything but straightforward. While some might view these platforms as inherently at odds with the principles of anonymity and privacy that define the Dark Web, others see them as complementary or even essential elements within the broader digital landscape.

- **The Dark Web's Influence on Social Media**: The Dark Web has the capacity to inspire and influence social media trends, utilizing its anonymity and security features to disseminate information and ideas that may be too sensitive or controversial for mainstream platforms. This interplay can lead to a blurring of the lines between the two spaces, complicating the task of discerning which narratives are being promoted on social media and which genuinely stem from the Dark Web.

- **Social Media's Role in the Dark Web:** Conversely, some individuals and groups harness social media to promote their activities or ideologies within the Dark Web. This relationship can lend a sense of legitimacy and visibility to these entities, potentially enticing more users to venture into the hidden reaches of the Dark Web.

The Impact on Online Activism

The intersection between the Dark Web and other online communities bears significant implications for activism and dissent. The anonymity and security features of the Dark Web make it an attractive platform for activists and dissidents seeking refuge from oppressive regimes and censorship.

- **Digital Activism:** The Dark Web's potential as a tool for digital activism is undeniable. It allows for secure communication and the sharing of sensitive information, empowering activists to organize and mobilize without fear of reprisal. However, this potential also raises concerns about the risk of co-optation by extremist groups or malicious actors seeking to exploit these platforms for their own agendas.

- **The Role of Social Media in Activism**: Social media platforms can play a crucial role in amplifying and supporting activist efforts originating from the Dark Web. They provide essential channels for communication, information dissemination, and organizational coordination, helping to bridge the gap between covert online activism and broader public awareness.

A Broader Context

As we explore the intersections between the Dark Web and various online communities, it becomes clear that these relationships are nuanced and context-dependent. The boundaries that separate different digital spaces are increasingly blurred, making it vital to approach each interaction with a sophisticated understanding of the complex power dynamics involved.

- **The Importance of Context**: Any analysis or discussion regarding the intersection between the Dark Web and other online communities must be grounded in a thorough understanding of the particular context in which these interactions take place. Different communities may have varying norms, intentions, and levels of accessibility that shape their engagement with the Dark Web.

- **The Need for Critical Thinking**: The ability to critically evaluate information and sources is essential when navigating these multifaceted digital landscapes. Users must remain vigilant against biases, misinformation, and manipulation, all of which can cloud judgment and distort understanding.

To illustrate the nuanced intersections between the Dark Web and other online communities, consider the following examples across different contexts:

1. Political Activism and the Arab Spring

The Arab Spring serves as a poignant example of the intersection between the Dark Web, social media, and digital activism. During the uprisings, activists used social media platforms like Twitter and Facebook to organize protests, disseminate information, and rally support. Concurrently, some activists sought to communicate and coordinate efforts through the Dark Web to avoid surveillance by oppressive regimes.

- **Contextual Nuance**: While social media provided visibility and quick communication, the Dark Web offered a layer of security. Understanding the socio-political climate and the risks faced by activists was crucial in determining the appropriate platform for organization and communication.

2. Protest Movements and Anonymous Groups

Groups like Anonymous utilize both the Dark Web and mainstream social media platforms to coordinate under the banners of various causes, from anti-censorship efforts to political protests. They often share strategies on the Dark Web while simultaneously engaging a broader audience through social media campaigns.

- **Diverse Community Norms**: The ideologies and tactics of these groups highlight the varying norms between online communities: the decentralized, often anarchistic nature of Anonymous contrasts sharply with the structured moderation on platforms like Facebook or Twitter. Each platform's engagement with the Dark Web can shape the differing methods of advocacy or protest.

3. Cybersecurity Forums and Darknet Markets

Cybersecurity professionals often use public forums to share insights, best practices, and warnings about emerging threats, which can include information about activities occurring on the Dark Web. Conversely, malicious actors on the Dark Web may frequent these same forums to gauge public sentiment or discover vulnerabilities in popular software.

- **Contextual Dynamics**: The interplay between ethical hackers and cybercriminals in this scenario illustrates the varying intentions of online communities. Different norms regarding acceptable behavior can lead to collaborations or conflicts depending on the context of the discussion.

4. Misinformation Campaigns in Intelligence Networks

Misinformation campaigns often leverage both the Dark Web and social media to create and spread false narratives. State-sponsored actors may utilize the Dark Web to develop disinformation strategies, only to disseminate these messages through social media networks to reach a wider audience.

- **Critical Evaluation**: Understanding how misinformation can traverse from an obscured Dark Web source to mainstream social media necessitates critical thinking from users. The level of intentional deception involved varies based on the source, emphasizing the need to critically evaluate information and discern its origins.

5. Communities Supporting Marginalized Groups

Certain online communities that support marginalized groups, such as LGBTQ+ individuals or whistleblowers, may use the relative anonymity of the Dark Web to share resources and advice discreetly. These groups often maintain a presence on social media to foster visibility and support while using the Dark Web for more sensitive discussions.

- **Navigating Accessibility**: The need for safe spaces, particularly for individuals facing discrimination, shapes how these communities engage with both the Dark Web and social media. The context of vulnerability necessitates a nuanced and cautious approach in navigating either space.

Each of these examples reflects the blurred boundaries between the Dark Web and other online communities while highlighting the many layers of context and critical thought required to navigate these digital landscapes effectively. Understanding these dynamics is essential for grasping the broader implications of the Dark Web within our increasingly interconnected online world.

Chapter 9: Ethics and Regulation

The anonymity afforded by the Dark Web has ignited a fervent debate over the roles of government and law enforcement in regulating this complex and often nefarious digital space. This chapter explores the intricate ethical dilemmas faced by regulators, as they navigate the delicate balance between combating illegal activities and preserving the rights to individual privacy and freedom of expression.

The Challenges of Regulation

Regulating the Dark Web is not only complicated but also fraught with significant challenges due to its decentralized structure and global nature. The very characteristics that render the Dark Web appealing to users—encryption and pseudonymous interactions—also hinder authorities' abilities to track illicit behaviors.

- **Decentralization and Anonymity**: The decentralized nature of the Dark Web, bolstered by technologies like Tor, complicates efforts to attribute actions to specific individuals. Anonymity technologies confound law enforcement's ability to identify perpetrators and gather crucial evidence, making it difficult to enforce existing laws effectively.

- **International Jurisdiction Issues**: The borderless aspect of the Dark Web further complicates regulation. Jurisdictional ambiguities arise when illegal activities span multiple countries, each with different legal frameworks and enforcement priorities. The lack of international legal cooperation exacerbates these challenges, allowing illicit activities to proliferate with relative impunity.

Government Involvement: A Double-Edged Sword

The involvement of governments in the regulation of the Dark Web presents a paradoxical dilemma.

- **Necessity of Law Enforcement**: Governments argue that robust regulatory frameworks are essential to combat illegal activities such as drug trafficking, human exploitation, and terrorism that find a haven on the Dark Web. Effective regulation can lead to successful law enforcement operations, the shutdown of illegal marketplaces, and ultimately, a safer society.
- **Risks of Overreach**: On the flip side, increased government oversight may inadvertently infringe upon individual rights, such as freedom of speech and the right to privacy. There is a legitimate concern that excessive regulation could lead to censorship or governmental overreach, stifling legitimate discourse, including whistleblowing and

political dissent that often thrive within this space.

The Role of Law Enforcement

Law enforcement agencies must carefully navigate the thin line between effective regulation and the infringement of civil liberties.

- **Ethical Dilemmas**: Agencies face ethical quandaries in their operations, often questioning whether the prioritization of public safety justifies potential violations of individual rights. The use of tactics such as undercover operations and extensive surveillance raises significant concerns. These methods can lead to accusations of entrapment, violate due process, and compromise the accountability of law enforcement actions.

- **Transparency and Oversight**: To address these ethical concerns, it is crucial to establish transparent operational protocols and oversight mechanisms within law enforcement agencies. Engaging the public in discussions about their activities can mitigate potential backlash and bolster public trust.

The Need for International Cooperation

International collaboration is a fundamental prerequisite for effectively addressing the global challenges posed by the Dark Web.

- **Common Standards and Guidelines:** Countries must work collaboratively to create unified standards and regulations that can extend across borders. Such cooperation will enhance the ability to combat global crimes and facilitate joint operations among law enforcement agencies.

- **Cultural Sensitivity and Legal Diversity:** It is essential for international regulations to consider the varied cultural contexts and legal systems of participating countries. This sensitivity will promote more effective cooperation and compliance.

Regulatory Frameworks: A Way Forward?

Developing a coherent regulatory framework that respects individual rights while addressing transnational interests is vital but complex.

- **Balancing Act**: Crafting these frameworks requires a nuanced approach that acknowledges jurisdictional intricacies and the differing motivations that drive users to engage with the Dark Web. Regulators must remain vigilant against creating laws that unintentionally criminalize harmless activities or silence dissent.
- **Engaging Stakeholders**: Engaging diverse stakeholders—such as technology companies, civil society organizations, and user groups—in the regulatory process can ensure that various perspectives are considered, helping to create more holistic solutions.

The Dark Web's Impact on Society

The Dark Web's influence reaches beyond its association with illicit activities; it is also a vital platform for whistleblowing, free expression, and social activism.

- **Legitimate Uses:** Many individuals rely on the Dark Web to communicate and share information safely, especially in environments where freedom of expression is heavily suppressed. It can serve as a refuge for those seeking to expose corruption or provide leads on human rights abuses.

- **Regulatory Complications:** Balancing the need to combat harmful activities while protecting legitimate uses is a significant regulatory challenge that underscores the complexity of oversight.

Personal Recommendations

To improve the regulation of the Dark Web while safeguarding civil liberties, several recommendations can be made:

- **Encourage Open Dialogue**: Foster ongoing conversations between governments, law enforcement agencies, and civil society organizations to ensure that diverse viewpoints are represented.
- **Develop International Guidelines**: Collaboratively create international guidelines that promote consistency in regulatory approaches without infringing upon fundamental rights.
- **Invest in Education**: Prioritize educational initiatives that raise awareness about the risks of the Dark Web while informing users of their rights and the potential for misuse.
- **Promote Global Cooperation**: Strengthen collaboration among nations to address cross-border challenges effectively, ensuring a unified approach to regulation that reflects

intercultural sensitivities.

The journey toward ethical and effective regulation of the Dark Web will require concerted efforts and a commitment to a comprehensive understanding of the interplay between individual freedoms, societal safety, and the diverse motivations that drive engagement with this enigmatic realm.

Ethical Case Study: The Silk Road

The Silk Road stands as a pivotal case in discussions surrounding the Dark Web, illustrating the profound complexities of regulating anonymous online marketplaces while shining a light on the ethical dilemmas posed by such environments. Launched in February 2011, the Silk Road was an innovative e-commerce platform that allowed users to buy and sell goods and services anonymously, utilizing Tor to conceal users' identities and Bitcoin for transaction purposes.

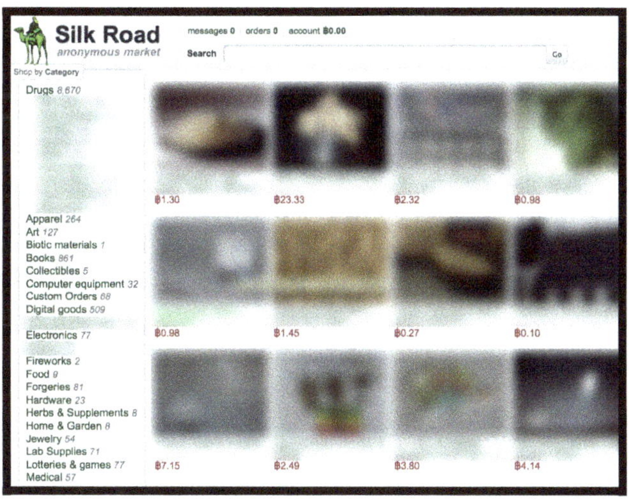

At its height, the Silk Road facilitated the sales of a multitude of illicit goods, including illegal drugs, counterfeit documents, and hacking services.

Its impact and subsequent shutdown have triggered widespread discussions about online anonymity, regulation, and law enforcement challenges.

Origins and Operation of Silk Road

- **Creation and Purpose**: The Silk Road was founded by an individual using the pseudonym Ross Ulbricht, who envisioned it as a free marketplace where individuals could engage in commerce without government interference. The platform enabled vendors and buyers to establish trust through a reputation system, providing ratings and reviews after transactions.

- **Facilitation of Illicit Trade**: While the Silk Road initially promoted itself as a means to support drug use in a safe and controlled manner, it quickly became a hub for all manner of illicit activities. By using Bitcoin, a currency that allowed for pseudonymous transactions, users could circumvent the traditional financial systems that often tracked and regulated monetary flows.

- **Censorship and Free Market Ideology**: The Silk Road also embraced a libertarian ethos, arguing against government restrictions and censorship. Ulbricht positioned the platform as a way for people to reclaim control over their choices, framing it as a socially beneficial enterprise while being fully aware of the potentially harmful consequences of the products traded.

Government Response and Shutdown

- **Investigation**: In 2013, the U.S. Federal Bureau of Investigation (FBI) launched an extensive investigation into Silk Road's operations. Undercover agents infiltrated the marketplace, gathering evidence of various illegal transactions. The investigation revealed not only the extent of drug trafficking on the site but also links to violent crime, including allegations of contract killings connected to Ulbricht's efforts to protect his business.

- **Shutdown**: On October 1, 2013, the authorities executed a coordinated takedown operation, which culminated in the arrest of Ross Ulbricht and the confiscation of the Silk Road servers. The website was seized, and law enforcement quickly published a statement celebrating the closure of the "largest illegal online marketplace." The shutdown was perceived as a landmark success in the fight against cybercrime, with law enforcement agencies heralding it as a major victory.

Legal Proceedings and Sentencing

- **Trial**: Following his arrest, Ulbricht faced several charges, including conspiracy to commit money laundering, conspiracy to commit computer hacking, conspiracy to commit conspiracy to traffic narcotics, and conspiracy to commit murder for hire—though no murders were proven. The trial commenced in January 2015 and drew extensive media attention, particularly regarding the ethical implications of Open Market vs. law enforcement intervention.

- **Sentencing:** In February 2015, Ulbricht was convicted on all charges and subsequently sentenced to life in prison without the possibility of parole. The severity of the sentence raised significant debate over how culpable Ulbricht should be held for the actions of individuals engaging with his platform. Critics argued that the sentence was excessive and highlighted the gray areas of criminal responsibility in the digital age.

Aftermath and Continued Appeal of Anonymous Marketplaces

- **Legacy:** The closure of the Silk Road did not eradicate demand for anonymous e-commerce; rather, it underscored the resilience of such marketplaces. Following the Silk Road's demise, several successor platforms emerged, such as Silk Road 2.0, AlphaBay, and Hansa, reflecting users' ongoing desire for anonymous transactions.

- **Increased Vigilance**: Law enforcement agencies worldwide have since intensified their efforts to regulate and monitor darknet activities. As new marketplaces popped up, strategies evolved with an emphasis on cybercrime units, cryptocurrency monitoring, and international cooperation.

- **Anonymity Technologies**: Users have adapted and developed increasingly sophisticated methods to maintain anonymity when engaging in illicit activities, leading to innovations in encryption technologies, decentralized currencies like Monero, and peer-to-peer exchange platforms which foster not only secrecy but also resilience against law enforcement efforts.

- **Presidential Pardon:** In January 2025, President Donald Trump granted a full and unconditional pardon to Ross Ulbricht, the founder of the Silk Road. This decision came after Trump had promised during his 2024 campaign to commute Ulbricht's sentence, appealing to libertarian voters who had long advocated for his release. Ulbricht had been sentenced to life in prison in 2015 for charges including distributing narcotics, engaging in a continuing criminal enterprise, and money laundering, related to his operation of Silk Road. The decision to pardon Ulbricht was met with mixed reactions; some viewed it as an acknowledgment of sentencing disparities and government overreach, while others criticized it, pointing to Ulbricht's role in facilitating illegal drug sales which had been linked to several deaths. This act underscored Trump's alignment with libertarian and cryptocurrency communities, who had campaigned for Ulbricht's release, arguing his sentence was overly punitive.

Regulatory Implications and Ethical Considerations

- **The Challenge of Regulation**: The Silk Road case exemplifies the inherent difficulties in regulating space that purports to operate under ideals of freedom, privacy, and the right to trade. While targeting illegal activities is essential, regulatory frameworks need to be cautious not to infringe upon legitimate uses of anonymity.
- **Moral Dilemmas**: The ethical questions surrounding the Dark Web touch on issues like the right to privacy, the role of government in mediating free markets, and the implications of censorship. Policymakers must grapple with the question of whether cracking down on illegal activities jeopardizes civil liberties and curtails individual freedoms.
- **Importance of Collective Wisdom and International Cooperation**: The globalized nature of online marketplaces necessitates international collaboration among governments, law enforcement, cryptocurrency exchanges, and technology companies. Crafting coherent policies and regulations requires a collective understanding of the cross-border challenges associated with the Dark Web.

Chapter 10: Academia's Role in Shaping the Future of the Dark Web

The academic community possesses a pivotal role in shaping the future trajectory of the Dark Web. As researchers, scholars, and experts, academics have the unique responsibility to contribute to the understanding and governance of this multifaceted digital realm. Their research not only informs public policy but also provides foundational knowledge that can aid law enforcement and civil society in navigating the complexities inherent in the Dark Web.

Understanding User Behavior

Academic research into user behavior is crucial for formulating effective strategies to mitigate the risks associated with the Dark Web. By exploring the motivations, attitudes, and behaviors of users, social scientists can generate invaluable insights that inform both policy decisions and law enforcement tactics.

- **Insight into Motivations**: Understanding why individuals engage with the Dark Web—be it for purchasing illicit goods, seeking anonymity, or accessing forbidden information—allows for more targeted interventions. Researchers can identify patterns in user behavior, helping authorities develop effective prevention strategies based on these insights.
- **Innovative Research Methods**: The inherent challenges of studying user behavior on the Dark Web, primarily due to the anonymity and encryption that characterize this space,

necessitate the application of innovative research methods. Techniques such as machine learning algorithms, social network analysis, and ethnographic studies can unveil patterns and trends within these elusive communities.

- **Ethical Responsibility:** Academics must also consider the ethical implications of their research. This includes ensuring that they do not inadvertently stigmatize or marginalize certain user groups. Researchers should conduct their work with integrity, fostering an environment where diverse perspectives are recognized and respected.

Technological Innovations

Technological advancements are rapidly transforming the landscape of the Dark Web. Innovations such as quantum computing, artificial intelligence, and blockchain technology are significantly reshaping what is possible within this digital space.

Academics are uniquely positioned to lead the charge in developing new technologies that enhance safety and security on the Dark Web. By exploring alternative encryption methods, decentralized networks, and other tools, researchers can facilitate the protection of users from potential exploitation.

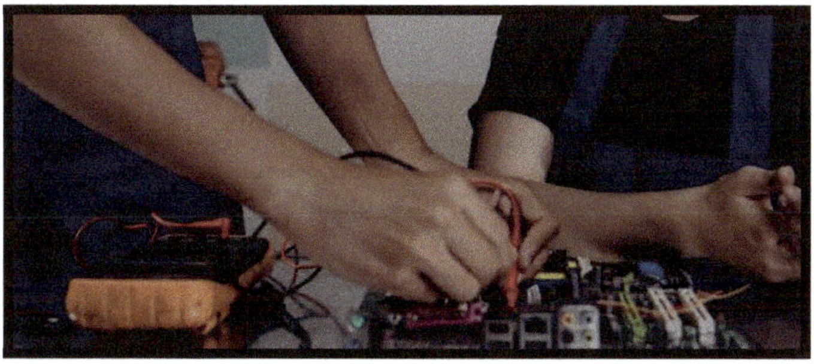

Ethical Frameworks

The establishment of robust ethical frameworks is pivotal for governing the activities within the Dark Web.

- **Guidelines for Responsible Behavior**: Academics can contribute meaningfully by creating guidelines and standards for responsible behavior on this platform. This could involve outlining clear principles for data protection, user anonymity, and cybersecurity best practices.
- **Engagement with Stakeholders**: Ongoing dialogue with policymakers, law enforcement agencies, and various stakeholders is essential to ensure that research findings translate into effective regulations and policies. This collaborative approach can help mitigate the risks associated with illicit activities while fostering an environment that respects individual freedoms.

Legal Scholarship

The intersection between law and the Dark Web presents a rapidly evolving and complex field of study.

- **Researching Legal Implications**: Academics can

provide profound insights into the legal ramifications of emerging technologies, focusing on how existing and proposed laws impact the functioning of the Dark Web. This includes assessing the outcomes of legislative measures and exploring how they shape user behavior.

- **Expert Analysis:** By conducting thorough legal analyses, scholars can inform lawmakers about the implications of their decisions on the digital ecosystem, ensuring that regulations are both effective and equitable.

Interdisciplinary Approaches

The study of the Dark Web requires an interdisciplinary approach that brings together experts from various fields such as computer science, sociology, psychology, law, and ethics.

- **Collaboration Across Disciplines:** By fostering collaboration, academics can cultivate a more comprehensive understanding of the Dark Web as a complex socio-technical system. This interdisciplinary approach will enable researchers to highlight new areas worthy of inquiry and develop innovative solutions to the challenges presented by this digital space.

- **Exploring Diverse Perspectives**: Including varied perspectives in research can lead to more holistic insights into user behaviors, technological impacts, and regulatory challenges, thereby enriching the overall academic discourse on the Dark Web.

Data Privacy Concerns

Data privacy stands as a paramount concern within the Dark Web context.

- **Prioritizing User Privacy**: Academics have a responsibility to prioritize user privacy while ensuring their research contributes to effective policy and regulation development. This includes safeguarding sensitive information, respecting user anonymity, and preventing potential data breaches or unauthorized disclosures.

- **Ethical Data Handling**: It is essential for researchers to adopt ethical practices in data handling, ensuring that their methodologies do not compromise the privacy of individuals involved in the study. Transparent communication regarding data use and participant consent is crucial for maintaining trust and integrity in academic research.

Personal Recommendations

- **Establish Clear Guidelines**: Develop comprehensive guidelines and standards for responsible behavior on the Dark Web, ensuring clarity in navigating ethical boundaries.

- **Innovate Technologically**: Focus on rising technologies that bolster user safety and security while exploring how these innovations can be effectively implemented in both academic and practical settings.

- **Maintain Ongoing Dialogue**: Promote regular engagement with policymakers, law enforcement agencies, and industry stakeholders to ensure that academic insights inform effective regulations and policies.
- **Safeguard User Privacy**: Commit to rigorous data privacy standards in research, ensuring that sensitive information is protected and that user anonymity is respected at all times.
- **Promote Interdisciplinary Collaboration**: Encourage partnerships across different academic disciplines to foster a comprehensive approach to the study of the Dark Web, leveraging diverse expertise to address its challenges more effectively.

Chapter 11: The Private Sector (Corporate Responsibility) and Market Dynamics

In the shadowy depths of cyberspace lies the Dark Web, an enigmatic and controversial realm that plays an increasingly pivotal role in the theater of modern warfare.

Warfare, as defined in this context, transcends the conventional battlefields of old. It now encompasses cyber warfare, information warfare, and economic warfare, each a battleground unto itself. The veil of anonymity provided by the Dark Web is a magnet for a wide spectrum of actors, ranging from state-sponsored entities to lone wolves, each seeking to exploit this digital hinterland to their advantage.

Cyber Espionage: The Invisible Battlefield

Among the myriad ways the Dark Web has transformed modern warfare, cyber espionage reigns supreme. An intricate dance of digital shadows, it is where hackers cleverly cloak themselves in the anonymity of bits and bytes, deploying techniques that span the arcane art of social engineering to sophisticated malware designed to penetrate and exfiltrate sensitive data.

The Dark Web is the hacker's playground, serving as a digital bazaar where tools of the trade are exchanged, vulnerabilities in systems are shared, and tactics honed. Yet, this treacherous ground is not just haunted by villains. Law enforcement and intelligence agencies are equally adept at using these very tools, perpetuating a never-ending game of cat-and-mouse, where innovation and adaptation are the only constants.

Economic Warfare: Veils of Anonymity

Shifting from secrets to finance, the Dark Web emerges as a harbinger of economic warfare. It presents a cryptic marketplace for sanctions evasion, money laundering, and a theater of financial crime that knows no borders. With cryptocurrencies serving as the currency of this clandestine world, offenders craft elaborate tactics to flout regulations and dodge detection.

Governments and financial watchdogs are embroiled in a never-ending conflict of strategy and counter-strategy, striving to keep pace with elusive adversaries intent on undermining global economic stability. This dynamic underscores the critical need for robust yet agile mechanisms to safeguard the financial ecosystem against the faceless machinations of the Dark Web.

The Role of Lobbying and Special Interests: The Unseen Architects of Digital Policy

Amidst the grim and convoluted landscape of the Dark Web, another layer of complexity emerges—one that is almost as shadowy as the realm it seeks to influence: the intricate web woven by lobbying and special interest groups. These entities, often operating behind closed doors and out of the public eye, play a significant and sometimes dubious role in shaping the policies governing the Dark Web.

Lobbyists and special interest groups are the puppet masters who tug at the strings of power, seeking to steer legislative and regulatory frameworks in directions that align with their specific agendas. These entities often represent a vast array of interests, from technology giants and financial institutions to privacy advocates and rights organizations, each with unique stakes in the cyberspace narrative.

The influence of lobbying and special interest groups on policy related to the Dark Web is profound and pervasive. It challenges us to rethink not just the regulations themselves but also the processes by which they are devised. By drawing back the curtain on these hidden dynamics and ensuring diverse, ethical participation, society can forge a more transparent and just approach to governing the complex, capricious nature of the Dark Web.

Collateral Damage: The Unseen Toll

Cyber operations, while often critically necessary, are not without perilous side effects. The unintended aftermath of these maneuvers reveals a grim landscape of collateral damage, where innocence is caught in the crossfire. It amplifies the urgency for accountability mechanisms, urging us to question the ethical implications of our journey into this digital battleground.

Chapter 12: Governmental Oversight: Regulation, Surveillance, and Ethics

The involvement of governments in the regulation of the Dark Web presents a paradoxical dilemma. On one hand, robust regulatory frameworks are necessary to combat illegal activities such as drug trafficking, human exploitation, and terrorism that find a haven on the Dark Web. But on the other hand, it raises concerns about infringing upon individual privacy and civil liberties.

Regulatory Frameworks

Developing a coherent regulatory framework that respects individual rights while addressing transnational interests is vital but complex. Regulators must navigate jurisdictional intricacies and differing motivations that drive users to engage with the Dark Web. Crafting these frameworks requires a nuanced approach that acknowledges the anonymity and decentralization of the platform.

Surveillance Tactics: Information Warfare

In the realm of information warfare, the Dark Web assumes another menacing guise. Here, it acts as a hornet's nest of misinformation and disinformation, a veritable Pandora's box from which propaganda and psychological operations are unleashed. Its untraceable nature allows shadowy forces to weave narratives that distort truth, sow discord, and rattle the pillars of democracy.

Governments, opportunistic factions, and

ideologically driven groups find in the Dark Web an unregulated channel to manipulate perceptions, incite chaos, and undermine societal foundations. This poses grave questions about the resilience of democratic processes, the erosion of social fabric, and the crumbling sanctity of media integrity in the age of digital warfare.

Governments have employed various surveillance tactics, some more ethically justifiable than others. These range from monitoring known illegal marketplaces to more controversial methods such as mass data collection. The use of these tactics raises ethical questions about entrapment, due process, and the boundaries of lawful investigation.

Ethical Governance: The Delicate Balance

The ethics of governmental involvement come into sharp focus when considering matters like surveillance overreach and potential abuse of power. Oversight mechanisms are essential to ensure ethical conduct. Any governance mechanism must balance security concerns with humanitarian considerations.

International Cooperation: A Global Perspective

Given the global nature of the Dark Web, international cooperation is indispensable. Bilateral and multilateral agreements can facilitate information sharing and coordinated actions against cyber threats. However, this cooperation also raises questions about sovereignty and jurisdictional issues.

Legislative Challenges: Existing Laws are Often Inadequate

Existing laws are often ill-equipped to deal with the unique challenges posed by the Dark Web. Jurisdictional issues complicate enforcement of laws, allowing illicit activities to proliferate with relative impunity. The lack of international governance mechanisms exacerbates these challenges, leaving many questions unanswered.

The regulatory landscape surrounding the Dark Web is fraught with complexities and ambiguities. Balancing security concerns with individual rights and freedoms requires a nuanced approach that acknowledges the ethical dimensions of regulation. As we move forward, it's essential to prioritize transparency, accountability, and cooperation among governments, law enforcement agencies, and civil society organizations to ensure effective governance.

Recommendations

- **Encourage Open Dialogue:** Foster ongoing conversations between governments, law enforcement agencies, and civil society organizations to ensure diverse viewpoints are represented.
- **Develop International Guidelines:** Collaboratively create international guidelines that promote consistency in regulatory approaches without infringing upon fundamental rights.

- **Invest in Education:** Prioritize understanding and governance of the Dark Web, academics should consider establishing clear guidelines and standards for responsible behavior on the platform.

Chapter 13: Civil Society and Grassroots Movements: The Power of the Collective

The Dark Web has long been associated with illicit activities, but it also serves as a platform for social activism, whistleblowing, and community organizing. This chapter delves into the role of civil society organizations in shaping the future of the Dark Web.

Advocacy and Awareness (CSOs)

Civil society organizations play a crucial role in raising awareness about the positive aspects of the Dark Web, such as its potential for social activism and whistleblowing. By shedding light on these issues, they can inform public opinion and policy decisions that align with broader societal values and ethical considerations.

For instance, advocacy groups have used the Dark Web to expose human rights abuses, promote transparency, and advocate for policy changes. This type of awareness-raising efforts helps to build a more nuanced understanding of the Dark Web's complexities and encourages responsible behavior among users.

- **Electronic Frontier Foundation (EFF)**: A nonprofit organization defending civil liberties in the digital world, EFF educates the public on various aspects of online privacy, including the Dark Web.

- **CyberWise**: This organization focuses on educating families and educators about digital safety, including the risks associated with the Dark Web.

- **TechSafety.org**: Run by the National Network to End Domestic Violence, this initiative aims to educate individuals about online safety, including the threats posed by the Dark Web.

- **Internet Society (ISOC)**: While broader in scope, ISOC promotes understanding of various aspects of the internet, including the challenges and opportunities presented by the Dark Web.

- **StaySafeOnline**: Powered by the National Cyber Security Alliance, this organization offers resources to help the public understand cybersecurity, including aspects related to the Dark Web.

- **Cybercrime Support Network (CSN):** Although primarily focused on victims of cybercrime, CSN provides resources and information about the Dark Web's relation to illegal activities.

- **The Anti-Phishing Working Group (APWG):** This organization addresses online crime, including phishing and other threats that can be linked to activities on the Dark Web.

- **Privacy Rights Clearinghouse:** This nonprofit organization offers information about privacy rights and online safety, including the implications of the Dark Web.

- **StopCyberbullying.org**: While focused on cyberbullying, this organization raises awareness about online risks that can extend to the Dark Web.

STOP cyberbullying

- **Webroot**: While primarily a cybersecurity company, Webroot also provides educational resources about internet safety, including discussions around the Dark Web's risks.

WEBROOT®

Whistleblowing Platforms

The Dark Web provides a secure platform for whistleblowers to anonymously disclose information without fear of retribution or censorship. Whistleblowing platforms, such as WikiLeaks, have used this anonymity to expose corruption, war crimes, and other forms of malfeasance.

However, the use of these platforms raises ethical concerns about the means by which they achieve their goals. The Dark Web's anonymous nature can also shield whistleblowers from accountability, making it challenging for law enforcement agencies to investigate and prosecute those responsible for wrongdoing.

- **SecureDrop**: Developed by the Freedom of the Press Foundation, SecureDrop is an open-source whistleblower submission system. It provides a way for reporters and news organizations to receive documents and tips from anonymous sources, with options for both regular and Tor network access.

- **GlobaLeaks:** An open-source whistleblowing platform that allows organizations to create their own secure and anonymous whistleblower systems. GlobaLeaks can be configured to operate on the Tor network.

- **onion.share:** A platform that allows users to share files anonymously over the Tor network, onion.share is commonly used by whistleblowers and activists to share sensitive information securely.

- **Whistleblower.org:** While not specifically a Dark Web platform, it provides information on how to report misconduct anonymously and securely. Some of its resources guide users on using secure methods like Tor for whistleblowing purposes.

GOVERNMENT ACCOUNTABILITY PROJECT

- **The Dark Web's WikiLeaks Access:** WikiLeaks itself has been accessible via Tor, allowing users to submit sensitive documents anonymously. While WikiLeaks primarily functions on the clear web, its operational presence on the Dark Web helps safeguard the identities of whistleblowers.

WikiLeaks

Human Rights and the Dark Web

The Dark Web has been used as a tool for human rights activism, with activists using the platform to coordinate protests, share information, and mobilize support. However, this also raises concerns about the potential for exploitation and manipulation of these platforms by authoritarian regimes or extremist groups.

To mitigate these risks, it is essential to establish clear guidelines and standards for responsible behavior on the Dark Web. This includes promoting transparency, accountability, and respect for human rights.

Community Policing

In the absence of centralized regulation, community-driven initiatives can help in self-policing the Dark Web. This involves reporting illegal activities and promoting ethical behavior among users.

However, this approach also raises questions about the role of law enforcement agencies in regulating online communities. It is essential to strike a balance between protecting individual rights and preventing harm on the platform.

Educational Outreach

Civil society organizations can contribute educational resources that guide individuals on safe usage of the Dark Web, targeting both current users and potential future users. This includes providing information about the risks associated with the platform and promoting responsible behavior online.

By doing so, they can help prevent the spread of misinformation and promote a more informed public discourse around the Dark Web's complexities.

Public Discourse and Policy Influence

Through advocacy and public discourse, civil society organizations can influence policy decisions related to the Dark Web. This includes advocating for policies that respect individual freedoms while ensuring accountability and transparency.

However, this approach also raises concerns about the potential for undue influence or manipulation of these discussions by special interest groups or authoritarian regimes.

In conclusion, civil society plays a critical role in shaping the future of the Dark Web. By promoting awareness, responsible behavior, and human rights, they can help create a safer and more ethical online environment. However, this requires careful consideration of the complexities involved and a commitment to transparency, accountability, and respect for individual freedoms.

Chapter 14: Advanced Techniques for Tor Users

As a seasoned user of the Dark Web, it's essential to stay ahead of law enforcement and other adversaries. This chapter will delve into advanced exploits and honeypots, darknet markets and darkcoins, understanding the risks and benefits, using cryptocurrencies safely, and listing some popular darkcoins that surpass traditional cryptocurrency options.

Advanced Exploits

Staying one step ahead of law enforcement requires a deep understanding of the latest techniques used by adversaries. This includes:

- **Zero-day exploits**: Unpatched vulnerabilities in software or hardware can be exploited to gain unauthorized access to systems.
- **Social engineering**: Manipulating individuals into divulging sensitive information through psychological manipulation.
- **Phishing attacks**: Using fake emails, websites, or messages to trick users into revealing credentials.
- **Honeypots:** Virtual traps set up within computer networks to attract, detect, and analyze unauthorized or malicious activities

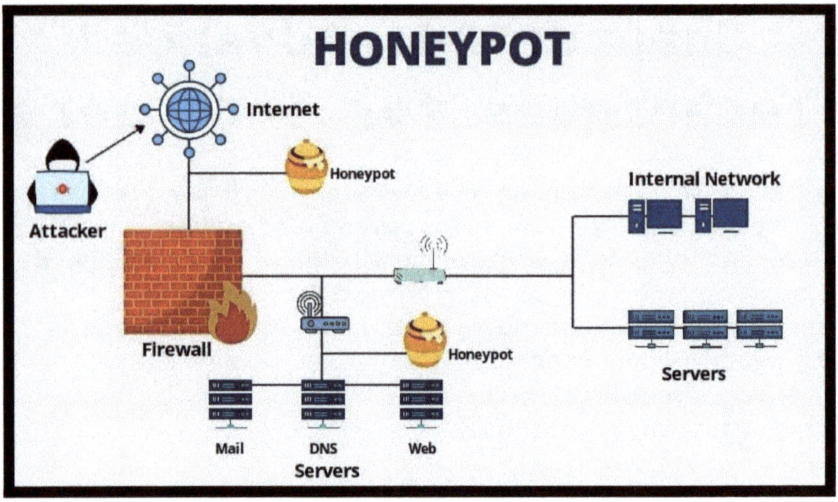

To counter these threats, it's crucial to:

- Regularly update software and firmware
- Implement robust security measures, such as two-factor authentication
- Educate yourself on the latest threats and vulnerabilities

Darknet Markets and Darkcoins

The Dark Web is home to various marketplaces that facilitate illicit activities. It's essential to understand the risks and benefits associated with these platforms:

- **Monero:** A cryptocurrency designed for private transactions, offering enhanced anonymity.
- **Zcash:** Another privacy-focused cryptocurrency, utilizing ring signatures and stealth addresses.

- **Verge (XVG):** Uses a combination of dual-key stealth addresses and RingCT (Ring Signatures and confidential transactions) to preserve the anonymity of both the sending and receiving parties.

When using darknet markets, it's vital to prioritize safety:

- Research market reputation and reviews
- Use secure payment methods, such as Tor-based wallets
- Avoid engaging in high-risk activities

Using Cryptocurrencies Safely

Cryptocurrencies can be used for both legitimate and illicit purposes on the Dark Web. To use them safely:

- **Use reputable exchanges:** Choose well-established platforms with robust security measures.
- **Monitor account activity regularly**

Some popular cryptocurrencies that offer enhanced anonymity include:

1. Monero (XMR)

Overview:
Monero was launched in April 2014, with a primary focus on privacy, security, and decentralization. It is often considered the gold standard of privacy-focused cryptocurrencies, primarily due to its strong features aimed at enhancing transaction confidentiality.

Key Features:

- **Ring Signatures:** Monero uses ring signatures to mix the spending signatures of a user with those of a group of users, obscuring the actual source of the transaction. This process makes it difficult to identify the origin of funds.
- **Stealth Addresses:** Each transaction generates a unique, one-time address for the recipient. This ensures that even if someone observes the blockchain, they cannot determine the recipient's actual address.
- **RingCT (Ring Confidential Transactions):** Introduced in 2017, RingCT hides the transaction amounts, adding an additional layer of privacy.

Consensus Mechanism:
Monero utilizes the RandomX proof-of-work mechanism, designed to be CPU-friendly and to enable mining using consumer-grade hardware, thereby promoting decentralization.

Community and Development:
Monero is open source and has a vibrant community. Development is ongoing, with regular updates that address vulnerabilities and enhance privacy features.

2. Zcash (ZEC)

Overview:
Zcash was launched in October 2016 and is notable for implementing advanced cryptographic techniques to ensure privacy. Developed by a team of academic experts and engineers, Zcash offers the option of shielded transactions, where sender, receiver, and transaction amounts are hidden.

Key Features:

- **zk-SNARKs (Zero-Knowledge Succinct Non-Interactive Arguments of Knowledge):** This cryptographic technique allows transaction data to be validated without revealing any underlying information. Essentially, it enables complete privacy for transactions.
- **Selective Disclosure:** Users can choose to disclose their transaction details to selected recipients or auditors while maintaining privacy from the rest of the network.

Consensus Mechanism:
Zcash operates on a proof-of-work model and has traditionally used the Equihash algorithm, which is memory-bound and requires significant amounts of RAM for mining, thus making it less accessible for consumer hardware than Monero.

Community and Development:
The Zcash Foundation and Electric Coin Company lead Zcash's development, ensuring a structured approach to feature releases and security.

3. Verge (XVG)

Overview:
Verge was initially launched as DogeCoinDark in 2014 and later rebranded to Verge in 2016. Verge aims to

offer complete privacy by utilizing multiple privacy-centric technologies.

Key Features:

- **Tor Integration**: Verge routes its users' IP addresses through the Tor network, enhancing anonymity by obscuring users' identities and locations.
- **I2P Support**: In addition to Tor, Verge also uses I2P (Invisible Internet Project) to further enhance the privacy of transactions.
- **Multiple Transaction Types**: Verge supports different modes of anonymity, allowing users to select whether they need their transaction detail kept private or not.

Consensus Mechanism:
Verge operates on a proof-of-work mechanism that allows for efficient mining, utilizing various hashing algorithms such as Scrypt and X17. This multi-algorithm approach aims to cater to a broader range of miners and promote decentralization.

Community and Development:
Verge has a strong community presence and emphasizes open-source development. However, it is often regarded as less sophisticated than Monero and Zcash in terms of privacy technology.

Additional Resources

1. **Books:**
   - **"Darknet: The Inside Story of the World's Most Wanted Man" by Zachary McKenzie**
     A look into the world of Dark Web marketplaces and the impact of the Silk Road.

   - **"The Dark Net: Inside the Digital Underworld" by Jamie Bartlett**
     An exploration of the hidden parts of the internet, discussing both the positive and the negative aspects.

   - **"The Code Book: The Science of Secrecy from Ancient Egypt to Quantum Cryptography" by Simon Singh**
     A historical overview of cryptography and its evolution, including modern encryption methods.

   - **"Permanent Record" by Edward Snowden**
     A memoir by the whistleblower that discusses government surveillance and the implications for personal privacy.

   - **"In the Age of Surveillance Capitalism" by Shoshana Zuboff**
     An examination of how companies manipulate personal information and its implications for society.

   - **"The Art of Deception: Controlling the Human Element of Security" by Kevin D. Mitnick**
     Insights into social engineering and cybersecurity practices from a notorious hacker.

- **"Cybersafe: A User's Guide to Buying and Securing Digital Devices" by Raheem K. Johnson**
  A practical guide for ensuring digital device protection and understanding various cybersecurity threats.

- **"Black Code: Inside the Battle for Cyberspace" by Ronald J. Deibert**
  Explores the intersection of technology, governance, and security in a rapidly changing digital landscape.

- **"Social Engineering: The Science of Human Hacking" by Christopher Hadnagy**
  Comprehensive guide to the tactics and techniques of social engineering attacks.

2. **Academic Journals:**
   - **International Journal of Information Security**
     Covers various facets of cybersecurity, including research on cyber threats and privacy concerns.

   - **Journal of Cybersecurity**
     A platform for discussing the latest research and developments in cybersecurity fields.

3. **Websites:**
   - **The Tor Project**
     (https://www.torproject.org) Official site for Tor, containing resources and guides on anonymity and privacy.

   - **Electronic Frontier Foundation (EFF)**
     (https://www.eff.org) A nonprofit organization that defends civil liberties in the digital world and provides guides on privacy and security.

- **Krebs on Security** (https://krebsonsecurity.com) A well-respected blog run by journalist Brian Krebs focusing on cybersecurity news and tips.

- **Dark Reading** (https://www.darkreading.com) A comprehensive cybersecurity community that provides industry news, analysis, and education.

- **Reddit's r/DarkNetMarkets** (https://www.reddit.com/r/DarkNetMarkets) A forum for discussions related to Dark Web marketplaces, safety tips, and experiences.

- **Bleeping Computer** (https://www.bleepingcomputer.com) A website offering a range of tutorials, news, and forums focusing on technology and security topics.

- **StaySafeOnline** (https://staysafeonline.org) A resource by the National Cyber Security Alliance that promotes online safety and awareness.

- **Lost on the Dark Web** (https://lostonthedarkweb.com) A site dedicated to helping users understand the Dark Web and navigate it safely.

- **Podcasts:**
  - **Darknet Diaries (Jack Rhysider)** Explores stories from the Dark Web and cybersecurity incidents, presenting interviews and narratives about hackers, data breaches, and the online underground. This is a personal favorite.

- **Malicious Life (Ran Levi)**
  A series that dives into the history of cybersecurity and hacking, blending storytelling with insights into how malware is developed and the people behind these attacks.

- **CyberSpark (Chris Marquardt and A. Harrison)**
  Discusses all facets of cybersecurity, including risk management, data protection, and emerging threats on the Internet—all relevant to navigating the Dark Web.

- **The Privacy, Security, & Anonymity Podcast (PSA) (Michael Bazzell)**
  This podcast covers a wide array of topics related to personal privacy, cybersecurity tools, and navigating the online landscape while maintaining anonymity.

- **Unpatched (Jacob Weston and Mike Kearney)**
  Latest in information security, discussing unpatched vulnerabilities and recent hacks, alongside discussions of software and its implications for privacy.

- **Security Now** (Steve Gibson and Leo Laporte)
  Covers topics in cybersecurity, including security vulnerabilities, privacy issues, and technologies related to online defense.

- **Hacker Noon Podcast**
  Drawing from the Hacker Noon website, this podcast features discussions with thought leaders in technology and

cybersecurity, focusing on innovation and privacy.

- **The Social Engineering Show (Chris Hadnagy)**
  Explores social engineering techniques, interviews with industry experts, and tips on defending against these types of attacks, which are especially relevant for those navigating the Dark Web.

- **The CyberWire (Dave Bittner)**
  Provides cybersecurity news summaries, insights from industry experts, and analyses on emerging threats, helping users stay informed.

- **Cybersecurity 101 (Andrea Little Limbago)**
  Aimed at all audiences, this show discusses essential cybersecurity concepts, dispelling myths and educating listeners on how to protect themselves online.

Glossary

Access Control: A security technique that regulates who or what can view or use resources in a computing environment.

Adversary: An individual or group that opposes or seeks to undermine the actions of another, often in the context of cybersecurity.

Adware: Software that automatically displays or downloads advertising material when a user is online, often bundled with free software.

Algorithm: A step-by-step procedure or formula for solving a problem, often used in computing for various processes, including encryption and data analysis.

Anonymous Communication: The exchange of messages or data where the identities of the participants are concealed, often utilized on the Dark Web to protect privacy.

Biometric Authentication: A security process that relies on unique biological characteristics, such as fingerprints, facial recognition, or iris scans, to verify identity.

Botnet: A network of compromised computers or devices connected to the internet that are controlled by an attacker to perform automatic tasks, such as sending spam or launching DDoS attacks.

Breach: An incident where unauthorized access is obtained to confidential data, compromising its integrity, availability, or confidentiality.

Burner Phone: A prepaid mobile phone used for a short period, then discarded to maintain anonymity.

Credential Stuffing: An automated method used by attackers to use stolen account credentials to gain unauthorized access to multiple accounts.

Cryptanalysis: The study

of analyzing information systems to discover hidden aspects of the systems, particularly aimed at breaking encryption.

Cryptocurrency: A digital or virtual currency that uses cryptography for security, allowing for decentralized transactions online.

Cyber Espionage: The act of using cyber capabilities to gather information from governments or organizations without authorization.

Cybersecurity Framework: A set of standards, guidelines, and practices to manage cybersecurity risks comprehensively.

Data Breach: An incident in which unauthorized access to confidential data occurs, resulting in potential loss, theft, or exposure of sensitive information.

Data Privacy: The aspect of information technology that deals with the proper handling of data concerning consent, notice, and regulatory compliance.

Denial of Service (DoS): An attack aimed at making a machine or network resource unavailable to its intended users by overwhelming it with requests.

Distributed Ledger Technology (DLT): A digital system for recording transactions in multiple places at once, improving transparency and security without a central authority.

End User: The final user of a product, system, or service, often in the context of technology and software development.

Encryption: The process of converting information or data into a code, especially to prevent unauthorized access.

Exfiltration: The unauthorized transfer of data from a user's system to an external location, often used within the context of a security breach.

Fingerprinting: Techniques used to collect information about a user's device or browser characteristics, often for tracking and identification.

Firewall: A network security device that monitors and controls incoming and outgoing network traffic based on predetermined security rules.

Forensic Analysis: The process of using scientific methods for investigating and collecting digital information relevant to criminal cases or policy violations.

Human Factor: The role that human behavior plays in the effectiveness of cybersecurity practices, often a key vulnerability in security systems.

Impersonation: The act of pretending to be someone else, typically used to deceive individuals or entities for malicious purposes.

Incident Response Plan: A documented strategy outlining how an organization will respond to and manage cybersecurity incidents.

Intrusion Detection System (IDS): A device or software application that monitors network traffic for suspicious activity and potential threats.

Keylogger: A type of surveillance software or hardware that records keystrokes made by a user, often used to capture sensitive information like passwords.

Malicious Software (Malware): Software intended to harm, exploit, or otherwise compromise a computer system, including viruses, worms, trojans, and spyware.

Master Key: A single key designed to open multiple locks or systems, often seen as a potential vulnerability in security systems.

Network Packet Sniffing: The process of capturing and analyzing data packets as they travel between devices on a network, often used in network analysis and security.

Operational Security

(OpSec): A process that identifies critical information to determine if friendly actions can be observed by adversaries.

Password Hashing: The practice of converting a password into a fixed-size string of characters, which is typically stored and compared in a secure manner.

Phishing Kits: Pre-packaged sets of tools that allow attackers to create fraudulent websites and emails to steal login credentials and other sensitive information.

Ransomware: A type of malware that locks or encrypts a victim's files, demanding payment for the decryption key to regain access.

Reputation System: A mechanism used on certain online platforms that allows users to rate or review other users or services, often used in marketplaces to establish trust.

Sandboxing: A security mechanism used to isolate running programs or processes to prevent malicious software from causing harm to the overall system.

Social Media Manipulation: The act of using social media platforms to spread misinformation or influence public opinion through targeted messaging.

Spoofing: A technique used to gain unauthorized access to computers or networks by disguising as a trusted source in communications, such as email or websites.

Supply Chain Attack: A cyberattack targeting an organization by exploiting vulnerabilities in external partners or suppliers rather than attacking the organization directly.

Temporary Email Accounts: Disposable email addresses created for short-term use to maintain anonymity online, particularly useful for signing up for services without revealing personal data.

Two-Factor Authentication (2FA): A security process in which the user provides two different authentication factors to verify themselves, adding an extra layer of protection.

User Agent: A string of text that a web browser sends to a server that identifies the browser and device being used, which can be manipulated for tracking or impersonation.

VPN (Virtual Private Network): A technology that creates a secure, encrypted connection over a less secure network, such as the internet, allowing remote users to connect to a private network securely.

Whistleblower: An individual who reports wrongdoing or illegal activity within an organization, often risking personal and professional consequences.

Zero-Day Exploit: An unaddressed security vulnerability in software that is exploited by attackers before the vendor is aware of and patches it.

www.ingramcontent.com/pod-product-compliance
Lightning Source LLC
LaVergne TN
LVHW052115210926
848482LV00025B/632
9798348478865